Ryan,

Much Love & Success

Auntie Cares You!

Thank You For you
Support

(signature) 2013

1

Here's the small print & legal bits and pieces…

For more information, please write to:
Kreative Publishing, Inc.
P.O. Box 562656
Charlotte, NC 28256
Phone: 800.511.5410
Email: info@ElyshiaBrooks.com

Kreative Publishing, Inc.
ISBN-13: 978-0615759029
ISBN-10: 0615759025

Branding the Authentic "You"

Building a Conscious-Centered Brand &
Lifestyle That Speaks To
Your Extraordinary Self

Author
Elyshia Brooks, MBA

Kreative Publishing, Inc.

Kreative Publishing, Inc.

My First Book is

Dedicated to my Precious Father God who leads and guides me and to my heart and joy, my son

De'Mon B. Brooks

All for You Babe!

Deuteronomy 8:18 – *"And you shall remember the Lord God, for It is* **He who gives you the power to get wealth,** *which He may establish His covenant which He swore to your fathers, as it is this day."*

Dedication

First of all, I **MUST** give my honor and gratitude to God, the Almighty! Thank you for entrusting me as a vessel to speak to hundreds, thousands and even millions to come. I Love You Father God!

For my dear family and friends who have supported me through conversations, prayer, encouraging words or even a listening ear; I really appreciate you. Especially, to my son, De'Mon Brooks who told me "You have got to want it bad enough…to walk out your destiny. You are the only one holding you back." That stung and pushed me to no end. Thank you son and I love you so much.

My family has stuck by me no matter what even through the dark moments. Thank you for believing in me, as you do not know how deep that touches my heart. I love you!

I have so many wonderful friends that I must say, "I honor you and I am so grateful for your accountability and encouraging words through the years." I Love You!

I would be remised if I forget to mention my clients from over the years. You have taught me how to be humble, creative and how to walk out my purpose. I could not do anything without you. To you, I will continue to serve and honor you as I walk in my authenticity and gratitude. Thank you bunches! It is because of you that I will live my EXTRAORDINARY SELF!

Contents

Foreword: Author's Note

Part I – Inner Work

Part II – Who You Are Called To Serve

Part III – Build Your Brand "You"

Final Thoughts

Resources

About the Author

Author's Note
My Authentic Realization

I know all too well on living on purpose and knowing what I am called to do, yet it has been quite a journey. When you really know your purpose and yet cannot get unstuck in your mind as to which direction to go, it becomes a huge challenge every day, at least for me. When I awoke every day and not know how to move pass the negative thoughts I have which kept me bound to non-productivity, it became a burden; especially when I could not get it out of my head and into fruition and manifestation. I know I am capable and able to make my passion work but I was constantly battling in my mind to move or not to move, to be perfect and to really not show up and play BIG in life! It has played a part not just in my life, but other people's lives as well. You see I have my story and my perceptions of things and so do the outsiders who thought they knew my story. After speaking with so many of my colleagues, business partners, clients and friends alike, it has become apparent I am not the only one who has fallen into this web, being stuck and no motivation to get out. Let me share what was 'my' story and how I have come to move pass what was holding me back.

You see I have always wanted to be an entrepreneur / business owner since my ninth grade year in high school. I was fascinated about being my own boss and calling all of the shots. I walked around constantly with my Entrepreneur, Inc., and Black Enterprise magazines and not to mention Essence so that I knew how to dress and look the part. My friends would always ask me, "Why are you always reading those magazines and what do you plan on doing?" My reply was "I am going to be my own boss one day because I refuse to make anyone one else rich when I can make myself rich." I was so serious and I studied what the successful people did and how they conducted business. Although, I knew that I would be my own boss but I did not know exactly what I was called to do just yet. I had an idea but it was not quite concrete; until I was in my junior year when I signed up for a DECA class with Mr. Author Horton.

When I got into that class, "WOW!" the light bulb came on and I was so engrossed in the class and fascinated by learning about business, marketing and advertising. I studied it and really fell in love with it. It was totally confirmed when I had the opportunity to be obliged by the presence of Dr. Rosa Okpara's marketing students from Albany State University who came to share with us more in-depth information on advertising and marketing, I was so engaged with learning all that I can about the field. I fell in love with the creative side and it was not until then when I was a freshman in college, I sat on my bed and heard a voice, Holy Spirit (or whatever you may call God) or my soul speaking to me saying that is your path, your business - Marketing. I knew from that day that I would be doing this in my life.

Now for those who ask me 'how did you know your purpose?' I knew in my heart what was and is what I am supposed to be doing; however, I begin to look at other interests such as event planning which I did like a whole lot. So I put down the marketing, but every time I would put it down, God found a way for me to pick it back up every time. I could not get away from it, even though I majored in Marketing with both my Bachelors and MBA, not to mention now earning my Doctoral Degree (D.B.A.) in Marketing. As soon as I accepted my purpose there were other avenues in marketing that I have explored because it is a complex industry; I have done a lot within it, but could not find my real groove. I realized that I had to go through some things to find my sweet spot. However, with the feeling of incompetence, not feeling good enough or smart enough; I began to doubt me even though I have my degrees along with the knowledge and love for it. How crazy is that? But the self-doubt would not go away.

I was in corporate America at a major bank working in marketing of course; it was then when I knew that God did speak to me about leaving very clearly and vividly. And until this day, I know, that I know, that I know, what I was supposed to be doing. So when I took the leap of faith and left my corporate job to do my business full time was so scary but I did it! I had clients, was happy and doing what I loved, but guess what the economy came crashing down and my clients decreased rapidly which caused me to go into what I call my "Dark Fog" of so many emotions. I became STUCK and actually paralyzed to where I would help others market and brand their business and I could not get myself out of that slump. Yeah, it lasted longer than I care to remember or admit, but I must be authentic and real. That is when I really went down and doing nothing and bringing nothing in. It really opened my eyes to a lot about me as a person, a woman, business woman, mother and a wife. It weighed heavenly on me that it did cause minor depression because I know what I am capable of but just could not pull myself up out of the mindset.

The emotions of self-doubt, negative self-talk, comparing myself, inner resistance, fear of failure and success, incompetence, low self-esteem, and so much more had been placed me to where it was difficult to get up, dust myself off and push pass myself to be who I was created to be. But now learning that I had to go through all of that and go around the mountain over and over again because I was not getting the lessons; which now I understand, so that I could share it with you. I resonate with my divine clients because I know where I have been and I know the work that needs to be done both inside and outside to be the person I was designed to do. Now I am living on purpose because now I really know what is fulfilling me and why I wake up every day ready and excited to empower others to move pass themselves and live the life that they were called to live. Also, I have the opportunity to provide coaching for my clients on authentic marketing and branding messages that speak to their authentic self. My road has been long and challenging. Now I want to save you time so that you would get there faster and not have to go through what I have. I have lost a lot of money and time until I found my true purpose and passion…**NOW I AM LIVING MY DREAMS AND MY PURPOSE!**

Do you believe that you are walking in your purpose, mission, gifts, or passion in life and more importantly business? How do you feel about walking in your purpose in your business? If you are wondering how to build wealth around your purpose, you must be committed to your happiness and living life abundantly We are being called to stand in our power and brilliance but there is so much "Stuff" and "Inner-Conflict" known as gatekeepers that keep you from showing up and playing BIG. Gatekeepers are the various energies that keep you from your highest and greatest good. So if you know the purpose that you are walking in and what is keeping you playing small; you must let that go. You cannot take the fears, failures and negative energy into your business and life every day. There are so many things that pull at us on a daily basis and at times every second of the day and you are not always aware of them and if you do, are you aware of how to get pass what is really holding you back? We all want to be successful in business and in life period but we allow "stuff" whether it's your thoughts, feelings, or the energy that we keep ourselves trapped in are our own unproductive thoughts; which is keeping us stuck right where we are in non-productivity. Have you thought about any of these questions for yourself and even how it would impact your business?

The End of Chapter Questions to Ponder

Answering these questions will allow you to look a little deeper as to why you are not putting forth an effort to market and brand yourself to become more visible. You must stop hiding from the world because there are divine clients in the world who need exactly what you have and if you don't put it out there, how will your divine clients find you? Stop perfecting things and get out there and once you get it out there, you can obtain feedback but you will never get that until you get out there for the world to see, like, know and love to work with. Don't let anything else hold you back from showing up in your life nor business that keep you crippled because you don't have the expertise, experience, education or anything else. The world is waiting on you...so it is time to show up!

NOTE: This book is based on some practical spiritual principles, in which you will see me reference 'God'. God for me is God, my Higher Power, Holy Spirit, Universe or whatever I see Him as for me and that may be different for you; but, for those who know that there is a higher power other than yourself, you will be able to understand the meaning of the book. You may call God whatever you call Him and are comfortable with. I hope that you understand that it is really about your soulful, conscious-centered heart that you read and hear from.

Introduction

The clear intentions of my first book is to not only share my story on how to build a successful authentic brand but to share with you that starting, owning and maintaining your dream business is NOT EASY! You know that you have the gift, expertise, knowledge and experience to start your business but there comes a lot of challenges and resistance that may keep you from showing up and living the EXTRAORDINARY life that you always dream of. You have made enough excuses not do it, but now is the time for you to come from among those who are "playing" business. I have been right where you are and was totally stuck, but I had to speak to myself and learn my own purpose and passion, not to mention my personal development.

This book has so much to offer by giving you clarity and insight on how to move past yourself, develop a soul-full, heart-centered, conscious minded, authentic personal brand and marketing lifestyle that will take you and your business to the next level. So I give you information on working on the internal self, get clear on what your true passion and purpose is and then build a brand that speaks directly to that which burns inside. But you must understand that you first must do the soul-work because if you don't, you will remain in resistance, conflict and blame because you did not get clarity. I wrote this book to touch the inner-self, your subconscious, negative self-talk and then change your mind set to from transactional marketing to authentic marketing and build relationships so you can work with your divine clients and loving what you do.

You will find something for every part of being an extraordinary entrepreneur, inside and outside, in both your business and in life. You are your brand always so you must wear it well. Your passion and purpose is what burns in your spirit or deep in your soul and you keep putting it down and picking it back up. I won't go anywhere and find its way back to you. Don't you deserve to be the best soulful business owner you know that you were created to be? I cannot allow my divine clients to have me believing in them more than they believe in themselves. I get really real and raw about my own story and how I have begun to overcome it. What is inside of you has to come out and when you do, you have to change up your whole mindset and shift from the old way of thinking to a transformational and an authentic lifestyle because your divine clients are connected to you.

I hope and pray that this book not only helps you to build an authentic personal brand but helps you to reflect on why you do what you do and enjoy it. So take your time to answer the necessary questions to get you started and if you need anything more…please don't hesitate to reach out to me. I will graciously respond and push you into your greatness to live your EXTRAORDINARY LIFE! Contact me at Elyhia@ElyshiaBrooks.com or visit www.ElyshiaBrooks.com.

In Your Success!

Elyshia Brooks

Chapter 1 – What Is Keeping You From Playing BIG in Your Business and In Life?

KEY CHAPTER TOPICS COVERED

- Your Inner Self Talk
- Money Mindset
- Playing BIG or Shrinking Down

Why Not Play BIG in Business and Life?

What have you thought about that is keeping you bound and stuck where you are in your business and also your personal life? What are the very things that keep you struggling, stressing, and fearful in being who you are and how you live your life? Perhaps, is it overwhelming, inner and outer conflict, comparing yourself to others, inconsistent cash flow; thoughts of incompetence, self-criticism, and your underlying belief that keeps affirming what you subconsciously live in lack of? Now I am only naming a few and not hitting the surface at all. Do you feel like you are spinning your wheels and not getting any further? Maybe it is time

You Live ONE life so Live It BIG! management, prioritization, not having the support system or the tenacity and energy to get to where you would want to be. Do you have the stable belief system that would keep you grounded to stay the course? If you would allow me to share with you what could possibly be some things that are keeping you from playing big and let's see how that resonates with you. I would love to share.

What does playing BIG mean to you? How does that look for you and what does success say for you? Playing BIG is different for everyone because what success might be for one is different for someone else. Success could be having an abundance of money, living a lifestyle that you always wanted, living in a big house and driving the nice cars or just even waking up in the morning saying "Thank You" for allowing me to see another day. Our thoughts and energy will have us playing small or BIG and that is totally up to you. Your life is depending on your mindset and how you would respond and bring BIGNESS into your life and all of that totally depends on you. So what does that really look like for you? Do you have any idea about how it makes you feel being in space living your dream and waking up every day EXCITED that you woke up?

Playing BIG for anyone is really walking in your purpose and living your life with joy, peace and happiness. You are honoring yourself to your core and living totally and completely authentically doing exactly what your heart desires. It is that *You come to live on purpose and to be as authentic as you can. Be true to yourself.* simple to live your dreams daily. What makes you so happy and joyful that every day, in every moment, you can make a way to do this regardless? You are clearing your life of all the environments and things that will keep you from doing it. You would work hard to be where you can see yourself; however, when we allow things and people to get involved, negativity keeps us from serving in our highest good. Allowing ourselves to really feel what we need to feel would open us up to get really clear and real with yourself and see what that exact thing which is holding you back. We have to embrace everything inside of us to embrace more of ourselves to know who we are, what we desire and how that looks for you to achieve it.

A lot of people have thought that they have failed too many times and cannot see how to be successful and those feelings of failure are crippling you. Your thoughts have become limited in where you want to be and how you want your business to be successful. You are maybe allowing those negative hindrances to speak louder to you than you need. What are the conversations that you have with yourself most of the time?

When we say things to ourselves that hold back it is mostly because of fear and as that fear and pain body grows taller and stronger, it becomes really hard to rid yourself of those thoughts. You need to acknowledge to yourself and say you are more than your negative thoughts and forgive yourself for allowing those thoughts to take root and let them go. Yes, that may sound quite simple and it is, but we make it a huge giant in our minds and in our lives that we just become stuck and do anything.

I must say that I am guilty of all of this because it is sad that we all have had to admit it at some point perhaps. For me, it was more of the negative thoughts and conversations I had with myself, not to mention so much negativity from people around me. My circle was relatively small but when there is an abundance of energy around you that is mostly of disbelief, I had to learn to rid myself from energy that was so draining to where I had to stop allowing it to keep me paralyzed in my tracks. I knew I had the education, knowledge, the expertise, and the skills to make it happen but my spirit and mind were not strong enough to move past the negativity that surrounded me and what was inside. My energy and life were not aligned at all. My circle of individuals who knew of me had more excitement and confidence in me than I had in myself. So when I speak from this place, I am all too familiar with this space. It is extremely hard to move past all of that if you don't work on yourself and change your environments. The desire and the tenacity have to be greater to you than anything else and you have to want success as bad as you want to sleep and eat. I know that I am not the only one who has experienced this lack of enthusiasm. We all have our good and bad days but how we move through them is totally up to us. Your destiny is waiting for you.

Express yourself authentically and ethically.

The limiting beliefs that we hold become who we are and how we view the world in which we live. Our experiences and perceptions are also what hold us back because of the circumstances that have emerged in our lives from which we could be holding on to. When we are ready to receive the abundance, lifestyle, and successful business, you will call that forth from deep inside and the doors will be ready to open because you would have aligned your thoughts and actions accordingly. We have all heard that when the student is ready to learn, the teacher will appear. The experiences that we have endured will either push us into destiny or keep us bound in a state of influx if we are not careful about dealing with our inner self. So are you ready?

Another reason that keeps us from playing BIG is that we are fearful of the unknown and that would keep us from starting, moving forward, or not doing anything at all. The unknown is just that, the unknown, it is all about how you perceive it to be and how you will chose to handle it. As we don't know what tomorrow will bring, so how can not knowing hinder you? Would that be the same in retrospect? How you think and how your thoughts contribute to your demise is a choice. We have choices and you can make the choice to become who you want to become in your own world and how you want to serve your divine clients. It is the relationship that you are having with yourself that will take you forward or backward. The unknown has kept people in bad business decisions, bad business relationships, and even a bad business because you did not follow your authentic self and be true to yourself.

There are no shortcuts to any place worth going. — Beverly Sills

What happens when you don't stay true to yourself and live totally authentic in your personal life and in your business? It challenges to lose yourself to that what you don't want to succumb and not living up to who you know you can be. When you don't live up to your highest potential, you begin to doubt yourself, your beliefs, abilities, and perhaps your future. Additionally, from a business perspective, one can lose the ability to be creative, become successful, and possibly have the loss of cash-flow.

If you look at your dreams in the face and it doesn't scare you, then your dream is not big enough. What do you ponder over that really scares you but you know in your heart that you are called to it? What gets you up every morning and is on your mind constantly? You know what it is and you cannot seem to get passed the hard work or the feelings that overwhelm your every thought. You are aware but you don't know how to handle what is

> *Success is going from failure to failure without losing your enthusiasm. – Abraham Lincoln*

expected and the magnitude of what it looks like for you. I am telling you to get pass that because you are supposed to be doing exactly that. Make up in your mind to do it and get it done! It is your time to be who you were born to be and you should be developing into your true self and not hold back under any circumstances. You deserve it!

One of the single biggest factors that keep people from moving forward in what they are called to do is the "Resistance". We all resist in different areas of your lives that keep us from being totally who we are. Resistance comes in various forms such as lack of inner-peace, reality, other's perceptions, power struggle, soul, worthiness, deserving, money, relationships, intuition, worry of finances, and so much more. You may have had a few to resonate with you but maybe not. It is totally different for everyone and how you deal with things that pertain to your environment that keeps you in a state of influx that is not bringing you to your heart-centered focus. Resistance really can cripple us from living an extraordinary life and reaching inner peace, power and a connection to yourself worth. If you are not cognizant of what that is, you are playing small and minimizing what you could be and should be doing. It takes you to look deep within to see exactly what you are and being totally honest with who you are and where you want to go and be. What is crippling you in your mind, heart or spirit that

Build your brand one person at a time.

you have to deal with and become present because if you don't it will show up in your personal and business life. It will keep raising its head in many forms that can show up in compromising your dreams and desires. Examine yourself and how you can change your thoughts to be even bigger.

When you have feelings of fear, lack, scarcity, envy, or worry, just to name a few, that you are contending with they can hurt you and keep you from moving forward. It is the negative feelings that are contributing to cluttering your mind and life so that you cannot be at your highest potential. As you think about the negative things or aspects of your business, you bring those feelings through your relationships with yourself and the clients that you may serve. Not to say that you will intentionally do anything to harm your business and clients, but the work that you put out may not be consistent with your brand by fulfilling your commitment. It can become really difficult to fall into a place mentally where you are in despair, especially if things are not on the upswing or cash-flow may be in the red. When you stay in that space, you will attract and bring more to you of that which you don't want.

Feelings and your belief system are things that you must change if you are going to create a business that is sustainable, in addition to having great people around you. But even with that you have to tap into your inner-self so that you know you are going to maintain what you were called to do. Your feelings amplify that which you are thinking and believing.

> *You may become the star of the hour if you make the minutes count.*

So as a business owner, it becomes the foundation where your belief system is rooted because that is what keeps you going, moving and getting up every day. It is something you should be attractive to you so you are able to do your best work and work with your clients that bring you more joy and happiness because you love what you do. As you go further in the book you will get a better understanding of that as you brand yourself and build a strong brand, you will be able see how your inner-self, consciousness in what you do will be intertwined in what business you operate and how you start and grow. You have not totally aligned your life according to what God has called you to and that is another reason why we are not blessed as we desire and should be walking in.

What Is It Going To Take?

What is it really going to take for you to move pass yourself and the stuff that you are holding on to be successful? Are there some things that you are having inner-conflict about or self-sabotaging thoughts that need to be resolved? What is it going to take for you to do some inner healing, self-awareness, and self-love to get out of your own way? It could or could not be a one day, one week or one month timeframe because it will take as long depending on the choice you make for yourself to work on you. It will take long for you if you are not willing to work at the self-awareness and go deep within to see the issues and challenges that are holding you back. You must get real down deep inside of your mind, heart and soul to face it, own it and make a choice to let it go never to pick that back up, including the emotions that are attached. I am not saying totally forget the memory, situation, or words that have hurt you but choosing

Build a brand that is known for "Giving" to own it and not allow it to have any more space in your mind and inner being. It is a choice that you make along with the commitment to yourself that you hold yourself to your own truth.

It is going to take you to change your mind set about where you are and where you want to be. It means that you will stop playing it safe and living below whom you are, which will cause to stop devaluing who you are and what you have to offer the world. The world is waiting on you get it right. They are waiting for you to walk in your power, your brilliance, and your gift and serve the world in how you and only you can serve it. You cannot make a choice to live below who you are. You must walk in your being and own who you are by taking back what is rightfully yours...your power that you were born with. The power that God gave you to walk in, in your authenticity is to make a difference in the world in which you were called to serve.

It is going to take for you to look within spiritually and honestly see what your inner-spirit is saying, directing and nudging you to do.

How many times have to be nudged in your spirit to do someth
you keep putting it down never really running with it, but it keep
back around? Perhaps that is your spirit telling again to do what you
called to do. You cannot get away from it because that is what you are
purposed for so stop running from it. Learn how to own your stuff and
that includes what you are running away from and become aware of
when those feelings tell you to walk the opposite direction what you are
thinking and how your body is responding. When we know that we are
supposed to do something
and we don't the energy in **A year from now you may wish you**
the body tenses up and you **had started today. — Karen Lamb**
may feel certain sensations
like some people get a sickening feeling in their stomach. That is Gods
way and your inner being telling you what you are supposed to be do. [7]
Learn to listen to your life!

You must do the necessary work to get clear, very clear on what
you were called on this earth to do. It is a spiritual path that you must
walk and being that it may be as an entrepreneur or business owner,
which can be a lonely winding road that is set up with doubt, confusion,
delay and a mediocre mindset. But because you are called to do your
sacred work in the world, you have to go through so that you can learn
you and become a better you.

End of Chapter "Points to Ponder"

1. What is really holding me back from living my authentic self and playing big or bigger? Be totally honest and transparent with yourself and love yourself through it.

2. What shift if any is keeping you stagnate and not moving forward? Identify it, own it and learn how to move pass it.

3. Do you have a great program, product or service and you don't know how to get it out and speak to your brand?

4. Are you having a challenge with your inner feelings that may need to be dealt with?

5. Are you totally clear about what you are supposed to be doing and how you are supposed to be serving?

Chapter 2 – Moving Pass Your Inner Obstacles That Are Holding You Back

KEY CHAPTER TOPICS COVERED

- Certain Obstacles That Keep Holding You Down
- Knowing My Purpose and Passion
- Getting Pass the Fear of Marketing

I Think I Know My Purpose, but I Don't Understand How My Authentic Self Serves the World

As entrepreneurs bud and start businesses from various industries believing they are walking out their passion and purpose but are clearly stunned when asked the question, "Are you serving the world as your true authentic self?" It becomes apparent they truly don't understand what it looks like or what it means. It is okay to not know because the majority of small business owners do not know. However, when starting a business or running a business, one must first understand their own sense of success and what it looks like for them and have a deeper connection to why they started a business fulfilling

> *Success is never failure.*
> *– Winston Churchill*

the highest and authentic expression of themself as they serve in business. Wow! How deep you might say, but you did not think of this when you were planning your business or you did but really never explored it deeper in this context of your marketing voice and how you present yourself to the world. Playing BIG in your business or expertise in this world is a huge expectancy.

Knowing your 'authentic self' as you navigate through growing a business takes many characteristics that should be instilled to separate you from the rest, such as *passion, truth, commitment, integrity, ethics, credibility, focus, simplicity, uniqueness, gratitude and joy*, just to name a few. Do you walk in all these or are you lacking in a few? Believe it or not, the answer comes as you operate in your business. These characteristics determine your authentic brand and marketing voice. If all of these are the driving force behind how you do business then you are walking in purpose and are ready to play BIG! Now if you don't own all of these characteristics that does not mean that you are not walking in purpose or ready to play big. It just simply means that you need to go within and pull out the ones that you are not as of yet and then work on them. It does not make you a bad business owner at all for clarification. Change is how you look at it and how you receive it. It is your choice.

Let's go a little deeper into the characteristics. It is important to know that when building your authentic marketing message and brand that you are creating how others view you and how you will do business. Therefore, positioning yourself as an effective,

> *Making a big life change is pretty scary.*
> *But, know what's even scarier? Regret.*

powerful and sustainable brand is vital in your perception of which you and your company are. It matters just as much to your potential clients as well as to your current clients and how they perceive you. Let's discuss.

The first authentic characteristic is passion. Passion is the most essential driving force of who you are and what you do because without it, there is no way that you will sustain yourself in business. Having a passion is what sets you apart from others. Because everyone is different and unique, there are many motives and experiences that drive our passion. Your passion is what wakes you up every morning and what you think about when you go to bed. You will think about it as you go throughout your day, because you are always figuring out ways to make things happen and be successful at doing it. Passion is a powerful and compelling emotion or feeling that anchors who you are. It is a sense of enthusiasm that gets you excited about learning and doing more. It is the force that pushes you on daily.

So what is your passion? What keeps you dreaming and thinking every day on how you can serve or what brings you happiness and joy? For some people, that is a really hard question to answer and to others, they know exactly what their passion is and how it feels. Your passion burns inside of you and you try to put it away, but it keeps coming back to you. Your life has a purpose and you are here for a reason and for whatever reason that is you have to find out so that you can live your purpose and have a strong passion for doing so. What do you think about all of the time? What are you always trying to figure out how to bring

The privilege of a lifetime is to be who you are.

more of that into your life? Are you passionate about the business that you started? Do you stay up late at night working on it? Whatever that is, is what you are supposed to be doing and you have that burning desire to make it happen. That's your passion.

When I sit with clients to discuss their business and what their marketing should look like, I am taken back by either the lack of passion or the deep passion that people have. At times when entrepreneurs are talking about their business and ideas, their passion oozes out and their face just beams excitement and a love for what they are doing or about to do. I love it because I feed off of their passion and energy. When I am sitting with someone who wants a marketing plan and they are so dry, I then have no energy to get excited about the work that I am about to do for them because I love and have a great passion for what I do that I just don't do it for money but to see their success and playing BIG! You see, when you have passion for something you want to do even if you cannot get paid for it. We have all heard of that statement but I believe it is so true. You will figure out how and the money will come but you have to take the first step to make it happen and take action every day.

When you have **passion**, you will live and breathe it daily which then speaks through your marketing voice and it eventually becomes your authentic brand because it speaks not only to you but in how you share it with the world. As your passion speaks through your brand, then your marketing voice speaks volumes to who you are supposed to do business with. Your passion has to be caught and it is an energy that you give off thus, your potential clients will get it and also feed off of you. What does your passion say about you in your business, marketing and brand? You must be clear on what that is to you so you can communicate that in all that you do.

Truth is an actual state of a matter with conformity or reality. It is a state of being true to you based on an actual existence that relates to integrity and principles. When one walks in authenticity, there must be some level of truth within so that you would not lose sight of what you are to experience and bring to any business. Your truth is what you live with that anchors you in who you are and what you

It's right to be content with what you have, but not with what you are.

believe about who you are. You see when you walk in your truthfulness, you are accepting who you are both the good and not so good as you know you to be. It starts with being open and honest with how you move through the world and what you bring to your business. Truthfulness is a moral position that tells you the facts about how you live, move and conduct business. It also speaks to who your brand and what it stand for.

Your truth is what you see when you look within. If what you know your truth to be in any experience, share with the world exactly who you are. You must choose to live and walk in truth in your personal life as well as in your business. In your business, your truth grounds you no matter what success you may achieve. This character trait says that you are living in reality and you can relate to others from a true state of being in other words, reality. When you walk in truthfulness, others can sense it and they are more apt to be trusting of you. It is said that in business, people do business with who they like, know and trust.

Walking in your truth means that you know that you know what you are born to do and you are grateful for the talents, skills and knowledge to serve in that capacity. Truth understands who you are and

Self-trust is the first secret to success.

what you have to offer without any opposition of fear and competition based on competitors. You are more of an original in your business and what you offer can transcend beyond you and your client's expectations, because deep inside you know your truth.

Commitment is pledging and engaging oneself in such a manner as a promise or an obligation that is always evolving. It is staying engaged and connected. What are you connected to in your business that keeps you committed to your passion and the truth that you live? Your commitment level shares a lot about who you are and your sincere promise to serving in such a capacity. When one is committed, they don't see the obstacles and challenges as a defeat but an opportunity to make a difference. As one becomes more committed to their passion, it shows and it makes the path a little sweeter. When you are walking in authenticity, you are committed no matter what the cause because it becomes who you are and what you are dedicated to doing. Can you honestly say that you are committed to living your passion and dream through your business and sharing with the world exactly who you are? If your answer is "yes", then you are looking to be successful regardless of what the circumstance may look like.

Integrity and **ethics** go hand-in-hand because integrity is living with the morals and ethical principles that build upon your character which is ultimately **honesty**. It is a state of being whole and undiminished in whatever you are doing. When an entrepreneur or business owner walks in integrity and conducts business in an ethical manner, it sets them apart from the rest. There has become so much corruption and unethical dealings in today's business world that it can be somewhat expected; which should not be the case under any circumstances. Ethics is having a philosophy for having values and walking in a righteous manner that people take notice of in all of your business dealings. It is what actions are right or wrong and how they come across in your business and how your clients perceive you.

> *You must TRUST YOU!*

In any business there must be **uniqueness** and **authenticity**, otherwise why go into business doing what someone else is doing? Your uniqueness is solely up to you and what you bring to the business and the experience with your ideal clients. Your unique selling proposition is what differentiates you from all of the others. It is a part of your business that your competition cannot say that they offer and it is unique to your brand and what it says about you. Our unparalleled and incomparable brand says that we are the only possibilities and solution that could help you with your challenge or problem. What stands out for you? What is different to your brand and business that no other person can say that they bring to the experience? We all have our own way of doing what we do because of the passion that we carry for what we do. We are all different in our makeup and how we think and do depends on who we are. We may have similar businesses, but there is a special uniqueness that separates you from the norm or from others.

Cindy Trimm, a profound speaker and high-impact teacher states that,

> "As we grow toward authenticity, our lives become more and more transparent, requiring us to rise to an ever-higher standard of accountability. Becoming more authentic, more genuine, more "real" requires a deeper sense of truthfulness, honesty, and honor. Our truest intentions are revealed. Our integrity is tested. Our credibility is established."

The ethical and moral concepts ascend from the motivation of what is noble, pure, just and honorable in all of its intentions and that transfers to all aspects of your life including your personal and business relations. When you live by such principles, you begin to *Your brand should include ethics.* handle things differently in your business and how you honor everyone and especially your clients because honor is what the basic premise is built on in relationships. Your clients must believe in you and they must know you are capable, credible and competent to serve them in the way that they desire. Ethics is a greater call to action to push you further into your destiny.

Fear of Not Knowing How to Market Your Business

Have you done several marketing strategies and you are not receiving the return on investment (ROI) from the marketing? Do you have a hard time putting into words what your authentic marketing message is to the world so that they know and understand exactly what you do? Or is your pain body one that keeps you tangled in self-expression in your business that does not allow you to show up in the world as your pure and authentic self? Are you not making the money from your clients and you want more high paying clients but don't know how to reach them? Or are you just not marketing savvy in your own right? And that is okay. Regardless, of what your marketing pain body may be, it is none the less, keeping you from attracting your ideal clients and not allowing you to do your best

> *Your pain body is what you identify with that holds you bound.*

work as you are not able to walk in your full purpose. As a business owner we need to really know our true authentic self so that we are able to share with the world who we really are through your businesses, talents, gifts, and purpose.

What is really holding you back from having the business that you desire to have? When it comes to allowing things, people, thoughts or whatever to hold us back, we are not allowing our true selves to grow and play big in a world that is waiting for us to show up and play BIG!! So we must identify with what that looks like for you and how to deal with it so that you can walk in your best self and have the business and lifestyle that you desire.

You Don't Know How to Compose a Marketing Message That Sets You Apart From Your Competition

Are you in a place of "Stuck" and just cannot seem to find your way through? Has your marketing message become buried in the filter of your competition?

We have all seen and heard of marketing and advertising that seeks to manipulate our senses, gets us to desire things that we either don't need or want, yet purchase anyway. Those marketing tactics have been the "way to go" for the past decades because that was the premise of advertising and marketing; getting people to purchase a product or service that meets a particular desire or need. Marketing has changed over the course of *Build true authentic meaningful relationships in business.* years from *product oriented* to *consumer oriented* to now *relationship oriented*. In the 1950's, marketing reflected the unmet needs and wants that was a source of value-based relationships. Now that we have moved to relationship and social marketing it has become more imperative to walk in authenticity to set you apart from your competition.

You understand that in order to do successful business, you must go with how the industry is moving or you will get left behind. In some cases; however, when it comes to the majority of the industry basing their relationship marketing on manipulative tactics to obtain more transactions than building solid authentic relationships there becomes a huge gap in connection between business owner and client. What does that really say about your business and the way that you handle your clients? There are many cases that businesses are now focused on the monetary transaction that does not lead to authentic brand loyalty and awareness. *The best strategy in today's market that yields the best return are those who are authentic in their own right and who are able to express their message to the world in a manner that would create consistent revenue.*

How is that really done? You may ask. It is done through communicating a clear authentic marketing message that would indeed speak to the heart strings of your ideal clients and speak the truth and not in a manipulative manner. Finding your authentic marketing voice speaks to your ideal clients in a style all of your own that says exactly what you want to say, the tone and the clarity of deliverables that say what you promise to provide.

What makes you different from your competition? What is your value proposition that clients are wowed about and keeps them coming back? Your authentic marketing message should share with the world exactly who you are and how you plan on serving them. As your business is branded, your clients and potential clients should know exactly what they will receive when they work with you. It should not be a surprise because they will know what to experience with you because they have connected with in your marketing. As your authentic voice arises, it opens the door for you to be who you are and they can connect with you and it makes it easier to engage them when they are in your presence.

There are a few strategies that should be included when designing your authentic marketing campaign that would create engagement and a connection to potentially open the door for new business opportunities. As a marketer and a business owner, one must understand there are various forms of marketing communications and channels that reach your potential clients. Each way yields different results. These forms include but not limited to *personal selling, advertising, marketing, social media and direct mail.* All of which are beneficial but how you use them with other marketing strategies my change the results desired. Your communication mode must be advanced and not dependent upon one particular channel. As a marketing coach, I always advise my clients to have at least 8-10 marketing strategies going at any given time because that is what will increase and boost your presence and identity at once. Some strategies may include the following:

STRATEGIES TO ATTRACT DIVINE CLIENTS

- You must make your "Divine Clients" feel as if they are Stars in your company by giving them a WOW Experience as they engage in who you are in business.

- Your expertise must give proof to who you are. The content that you provide is stellar and purposeful to your divine clients and that you are connecting with them on a level that is appropriate to them to understand and can appreciate by finding you valuable.

- You should create content and programs that will speak to their heart strings and assist in solving their challenges and problems. This includes blogs, newsletters, programs, services and products that they can use and implement because it has become crucial for them to have.

- As you grow your business and followers you would need to look at how you continuously keep them engaged with your messages, frequency, various channels, content and then ultimately your conversation with them. You have to speak to them right where they are and really speak "to" them and not "at" them. It is important on how you communicate with them because, that is the biggest connection piece.

- Promote your content, brand and information on all of the social networks. Use the social media outlet as your friend and your platform because that is where your business receives exposure. Remember that some social media does not have a huge ROI (Return On Investment) in terms of financial but that depends on how you use it. It is rewarding in building strong relationships that could yield short and long-term success and profits. It really does create brand identity and equity.

- Open the door to increasing your platform by becoming an expert in your field where you are recognized as an "Authority" in your industry. When you speak there are many who take notice on what you have to say and can appreciate you. This opens the doors for you to have media exposure and speaking engagements and many other things that create opportunities.

- Increase your "Likeability," "Followers" and Fan Page "Likes" because this gives you access to many open referrals and exposure that you would not have had otherwise. It is the most single thing that you can do to build your brand and that is not expensive. So why not participate. It is said that if business owners are not participating in social media, they will be left behind.

Business Example

What it looks like for you in your business may be totally different than in someone else's, because you have different goals and a different purpose that makes you unique. For instance, I have two clients who potentially do the same business but how they market it is totally different. Both of them are very good in what they do and I do believe that it is their passion and purpose; however, their marketing message and brands are different. They both cater to non-profit organizations and offer professional seminars, so one day I was asked by both to come and observe their seminars and offer my feedback on the marketing, their brand and their overall presentations. I was taken back by what I saw because they are both good at what they do. So let me explain what I observed and relate it back to their brand which we know is ultimately "you".

For the sake of it, let's call them Professional #1 and #2, not in any order by any means. The Professional #1 was working her business and her brand, at least I thought until I was able to observe. First, they both charged a flat fee of $99 for their workshop that was targeted for non-profit start-ups. I walked into the hotel where they held the workshop; and I immediately noticed that the presenter had not arrived as I did arrive thirty minutes early as always. Her assistant was there checking the attendees in and giving them the agenda for the day. I counted in 27 individuals who had paid to attend and all of them did show up. I asked my client's assistance where my client was and she mentioned that "she was running late and that she was on her way." I looked at my watch and it was then about fifteen minutes prior to the start time and she had not arrived, so I went in and networked with the attendees and asked how did they hear about the seminar and what caught their attention. They provided very honest answers which ranged from, just starting up and need some direction to I am ready to build my non-profit and the emails peeked their interest to attend; which the marketing was very professional and it spoke directly to the target market.

41

As I took my seat in the back so that I could observe better, I noticed the presenter comes in frazzled and frantic because she was late and this was, I know to be just not who I perceived her to be in the office and doing business. Another huge observation that took me by surprise was that they were dressed in "jeans" and a nice blouse, which is a BIG NO NO! I did not say anything at the moment but just observed. She provided excellent material and information that really showed who she was on paper, yet in her presentation, she did really well, in other words, she knows her stuff, with no doubt. However, the workshop was supposed to last from 9-4, but at the first break which was like an hour and half into the workshop, I noticed two people did not come back into the workshop, which I notated. I observed another nine people leave during the lunch break and did not return which I caught most of them as they were on the way out and they mentioned that "I paid $99 to attend a workshop and the information is good, but I cannot get passed how unprofessional she looks, how can anyone take her seriously even with this great information? I can figure it out or find someone else who is professional." Wow, they were very blunt!

After this workshop, I did sit with her and shared my thoughts, observations and as well as the attendee's concerns. She was astonished at the comments and felt really bad about the entire experience even though she provided a great presentation. I shared with her that she "is" her brand and that she is marketing herself and her business every time she is in front of clients and potential clients. How she presents herself speaks volumes to others and how they perceive you and if they are going to do business or repeat business. Now, some say that was a little extreme, but not in the small business world and growing as an entrepreneur, it may be crucial and it will come down to the fact do they like, know and trust you enough to do business.

My other client had a similar workshop geared towards non-profit directors as well and it was the total opposite. She arrived on time, actually an hour or so ahead of time and was dressed professionally. She had roughly thirty-five people in attendance and she did not have anyone to leave because she had the tools and the information to keep them engaged and her presentation was really good. She seemed to know as well as the other client, her profession, her material and her industry. The particular aspects of her business were as noticeable because she seemed to have the ultimate passion for what she does.

I mentioned this story because when you know your purpose and you have passion for what you do, you will take your brand seriously. The difference in the two business owners was that they had different marketing mindsets and how they view their business. When one has strong values and pride in how they operate their business, it speaks for you. It shows in the way that you conduct and handle your business. There is a difference in owning a business and operating a business. If you have authentic joy and you wake up daily excited about doing what you do, it will show in everything that you do and how you brand yourself. Now, since then, the Professional #1 has changed her marketing mindset and really has taken a look at what needed to be changed and how it can affect her brand, but it was a learning lesson for her and my other clients.

Don't Know How to Authentically Put Your Business into Words That Attract Your Ideal Clients

There are many business owners and entrepreneurs who have very different marketing messages that don't portray the real brand that they intended for their target audience to receive. The message gets cluttered in what maybe should not be intertwined in the brand. Your positioning statement should be what you stand for and what you represent and the words that you use are supposed to attract and some just really don't understand the connection between the two. When one has this grand "Aha Moment" about their business idea and what it will look like but they don't know how to put the words out there to attract their ideal clients, it becomes overwhelming. One must put in authentic strong selling points that would share the values and personality of your brand.

Creating an authentic marketing message that will remain consistent throughout the mediums is important. Having an authentic message should be at the core of your business brand and what the business stands for. It may come as confusing to many on how the message should convey the brand and the value proposition that it stands for. The approach can be voiced as strong, calm, creative, and traditional or whatever you want your brand to stand for, but it must be clear and represent you. As potential clients are bombarded with increased noise, advertising clutter and various choices on to fight through, there must be something about you and your business that stands out above the rest. Your marketing message has to pull at their heart strings consistently for them to resonate with your brand, in other words, you have to talk their language and speak to their marketing pain body.

As you design your marketing message it is to be understood that as you compose it that your ideal clients will hear it and resonate with it because that is what they need as a solution for a particular challenge. Once you recognize what you want to accomplish in your message first because that is the ultimate message that the world will relate with. If you have multiple marketing messages it will become confusing for your clients and they would not know what to call you for and exactly what services you can assist them with. It must be clear and understood so that there are no misconceptions. With the community being bombarded with so many ads, messages, communities and the like, they are becoming more specific in who they do business with and if they are going to receive exactly what they are promised. This is when the client is attracted to the marketing message, because it speaks directly to them; so it has to be appealing and unique. It is said that we are bombarded with 3500-5000 ads per day via the television, radio, billboards, and magazines and so on. Therefore, to get through all of that clutter, your marketing message must trigger a *pain body* that would provoke action from your ideal clients.

As you evolve in your business, the marketing message and branding would remain the same unless you are rebranding and starting another business. Your marketing message should remain exactly what it is because if it is constantly being changed, your clients will become confused and the brand loyalty may drop. As the marketing message is consistent and is stated with great understanding, then it is most likely to be remembered.

Inner Work Begins Here & Now

As you grow as an entrepreneur and business owner, one must understand their inner being and the core of who they really are as an individual. You have cleaned out the clutter and moved pass what has been holding you back. I guarantee if you don't do the work now and learn from it, the lesson that you need to learn about yourself will keep reappearing until you get it. That is just the Law of Attraction and Cause and Effect. You cannot get away from it. So really get with yourself right now and do the necessary work to ask the tough questions while being totally honest with you because no one is looking BE HONEST and TELL THE TRUTH! Let's get started. ....

What are your passions and desires? List them below.

_____

_____

_____

_____

_____

_____

_____

_____

_____

What do you want more of? Better Health? Abundance? Wealth? Purpose and Passion?

_____

_____

_____

_____

_____

_____

What is the connection that you have to a Higher Source? This is very, very important to how far you may go.

_____

_____

_____

_____

_____

_____

What energy are you giving of that is keeping you from attracting your ideal clients? Be Honest!

_____

_____

_____

_____

What is most important to you right now today? What is your Big WHY?

_____

_____

_____

_____

_____

_____

_____

What does your spirit really tell you about the path that you are walking in?

_____

_____

_____

_____

_____

_____

How can you give and serve others?

_____

_____

_____

_____

_____

What are your intentions? Get really clear.

_____

_____

_____

_____

_____

_____

What causes to you stand up in who you are to the world and know your stuff?

_____

_____

_____

_____

_____

What is the ultimate goal that you want to accomplish?

_____

_____

_____

_____

_____

_____

<u>End of Chapter "Points to Ponder"</u>

1. What is truthfully holding you back from fully marketing you and your business?

2. What are you afraid of that people may find out if you had to be totally honest with yourself?

3. When you market yourself, you know that you have to show up in a huge way, so what is keeping you from showing up doing what you know that you were born to do?

4. If you are lacking the marketing skill set, then what is holding you back from hiring a marketing coach and getting it done?

5. If you had an unlimited marketing budget what would you do to best market you and your brand?

6. What are the top three things that are keeping you from becoming more visible in your industry and playing big?

7. What is the marketing and brand message that you want to share with the world about what you do?

8. Do you look at others marketing and compare yours to theirs which causes you to become stuck and always changing your materials?

9. Are you a perfectionist in everything which includes your marketing to the point where you are not giving anything out?

10. If you set a date to begin your marketing campaign, what date would that be?

Chapter 3 – Finding Your Unique Authentic Voice to Share with the World

KEY CHAPTER TOPICS COVERED

- How To Find Your Unique Authentic Voice
- Designing a Marketing Message That Speaks Directly To Your Divine Clients
- Figuring Your Purpose and Passion

What is the Message You Want to Share with the World?

Your authentic marketing message it what you shout to the world about what you do, what your business has to offer and how you play BIG in your authentic space. When you are pursuing your passion and purpose, you should know how to communicate that to the world; however, some don't know how to or they get stuck on what it should say that attracts clients consistently. What you say and how you say it speaks volumes to your clients and your industry, so it should be simple, concise and come from the core of your soul about your business. The marketing message should also flow throughout your entire marketing, branding and communication strategies. When you know your targeted niche, (divine clients), you can speak directly to what they are in need of which captures them through an effective and soulful message. What you shout to the world should be strong and effective, yet speaking with confidence that your business is a conscious-centered business that is heart-centered. The more concise your message is the better targeted it is, which makes the approach much simpler.

When one is trying to find their authentic voice, there must be some self-discovery that should take place in order to experience and explore the true essence of who they are and what really is significant in walking out their purpose and how it relates to their business. Your purpose, passion and destiny are interconnected and they play out in your personal life and your business. But most significantly, you have a true authentic joy in what you bring to the experience which is peace and harmony in your life and in your business. They both are interdependent

53

on the other because your business is built on a solid foundation of your values that are intertwined in your lifestyle and how you live your life. You bring joy to both, which is ultimately living authentically because you are doing what brings you joy, peace and happiness. When you can live in both worlds as authentically as you can, that says a lot because you cannot live your passion freely and be bottled up.

When you begin to share with the world exactly who you are, you must begin by telling your story. Your story is your experience which you have lived and you can give insight on how you went through that experience and what you did to get out of where you were. That story is what you tell from your heart and your divine clients can relate to you and put themselves in your shoes as you have placed yourself in theirs.

Transform your life by the words that you speak about "You"!

It is how you speak to their pain body and what gets them hooked on the solutions that you can provide. When a client reverberates with you, they are more understanding and can see you use a significant process that is to better enhance their life or business in a certain way. You perfect your process and systems for your clients that yield results consistently; therefore, they can then offer you testimonies based on having worked with you and have proven that what you have done really does work. It is not about convincing the clients but it is about telling the truth of how it worked and what the actual outcome really is. When you are telling the truth it means being sincere and honest with what works and doesn't work. It comes with the understanding that the outcomes could be different for others because all of the clients have different and unique challenges that may or may not result in the same way. Moreover, there are times when clients don't receive the same results because they may not do things the same way as others but for the most part the process continues to work. In which case, this ultimately relates back to your authentic brand.

Learning How to Speak What You Do So Others Understand

An authentic marketing message speaks directly to your niche and they understand exactly what you are saying because it grabs their attention to your offer based on your service or product. It grabs their attention and their ability to relate to where there are no questions about your product or service and how it is exactly what they need and it will bring them the results they have been seeking. However, when you're *Decide to speak to someone new every day about your authentic message.* developing a marketing system and process to speak their language, it will come to you and it will pull them in and attract them because you are answering their questions and resolving their challenges. The message is authentic, clear and concise for their needs.

When you speak to the pain body of your niche they are able to catch and grab it so there is a resonation with your offer and it will solve exactly what they are looking for. However, your marketing voice needs to speak their language and it is at the very core of your soul that creates an attachment which pulls the client in to where they would want to see what you can do specifically for them. There are several people and potential clients that have similar challenges, yet they cannot articulate it, but when they hear it through your authentic marketing message clearly, then it will trigger what they are challenged with and prompts them to call you to inquire. Sometimes, it's not until you put your marketing message out into the world and your divine clients read it, understands it, and connects with it, so that you will gain their interest. This is why your marketing message has to be unblemished and crisp to speak directly to them.

Your marketing message is in direct correlation with who you are and your purpose in what you provide and when you are serving in a capacity, you are providing exactly what you are supposed to, *Your authentic message should* to whom you are supposed to serve. There should be no question about what it is that you do and you know you do it well. But the question becomes how do you know what message to put out there that would grab hold of your clients? Their pain body is what you are speaking to and that is the solution that you will provide because that is your expertise and only you can do it like you do. Your brand message and your soulful brand is what you bring to the center of your business and that's what you become known for and build your brand as an expert on your particular knowledge and experience.

In order to speak to your divine clients, you must first identify with them and meet them right where they are in their need. This is done by asking a few questions that would give you clarity and what you should offer and who would purchase your products or services. The question consists of the following:

1. What is the language that you need to speak to grab their attention?
2. Who is authentically drawn to you that they get you? Your business, personality and your purpose?

3. Who are you drawn to work with and are able to do your best work?

4. Who consistently finds your service or products valuable and appreciates you and your business?

5. What problems does your potential clients have that you have the solutions to?

Your marketing niche has to be refined and solve the anxieties of others and when you know that, you can consistently bring positive results over and over to the same problem. When you make it your positioned brand and purpose, it can create a successful business. It becomes a process and you have to be willing to endure the process because it is not always going to come easily to you, but you should know that you are honoring who you are as you serve in your capacity.

What is Your Purpose, Passion and Plan for Your Business?

Often times I am questioned, "How do you know if you are walking in your purpose and how does it bring you joy?" I use to be taken back by how to answer this question because I was not always sure or quite comfortable with what I was doing because like many, I felt inadequate and at times incompetent because of my own personal feelings. We all have had our times of those feelings and it is quite normal, but what I have found out from my own experience and from others is that if you keep putting whatever that is down and you continue to find yourself going back to it, then you need to explore it and seek direction about that being your purpose. God, Universe or whomever you may call your Higher Being is directing and guiding you towards that particular talent or gift. Your purpose has been shared with you but it is

57

up to you to become aware and realize what it is and walk in that direction.

I often ask, "What brings you the greatest joy when you are doing something?" What makes your heart simile when you see the results of your efforts and you are serving clients who love what you provide? It is hard for some to find what really brings joy to people and make money at the same time. It is really about creating a business that serves your higher purpose and what ultimately brings you joy and peace, so much that you wake up thinking how to do it better. When you begin to combine your attention and your authentic creativity to birth what you are purposed to do, your existence becomes meaningful and impacts more than just you. When you're doing what you are called to, you attract those who are supposed to work with you naturally. It is said by Rumi, "Let yourself be silently drawn by the stronger pull of what you really love." I guarantee that you will not be fulfilled until you finally do it. But you first must ask the question, "Do I really love what I am doing?" As you become more centered you will begin to pursue your passion and the money will follow.

Your purpose is always connected with what God has planned for you and how you are to operate in your business and personal life. It is all connected together from a spiritual point of view. Therefore, your business is more given towards the gifts and talents that you were born with. Your passion burns inside and it pushes your motivation to succeed even more. When your passion and purpose are united, it then creates a goal to go after and serve the world regardless of what obstacles may come. When you are passionate about what you do and you love it, then it becomes a part of you and it finds a place in your business model. Your passion pushes you into greatness as long as you are pursuing it and that is your focus and commitment. The passion you are pursuing, you cannot get away from it and it is what will bring you more joy. Your passion and gifts make room for you and because you are called to that, then you are to be successful in it and He will make your name great.

When you are walking in your purpose and passion, you are operating at your highest good because it brings you to a sense of being as you are doing what you love. It absolutely feeds your soul. Some may have different passions other than you and that is okay; however, you can only do it the way that you do it. Passion is what you will find to do that may or may not bring you the lifestyle that you have always dreamed, based on your actions. There are many businesses that have started from the passion of doing something. There are creative ways to make money from your passion; however, it would need to be planned and thought out. You can build a business from so many things that come from a thought and there is only one way to know and that is to "try." Whatever you do, don't give up on your passion and purpose in life.

How Do You View Yourself and How You Want Others to See You and Your Business?

"You" are your "Brand" and how you view yourself plays a major role in how others see you and your business. When you decide to build a business you should begin thinking about what you want to be known for in your industry and the how you want to play BIG in the world. As you decide on what you want to communicate and how, that is what your brand will consist of. As entrepreneurs blossom, there is a greater need to just be known as someone starting a business and someone who really just wants business, but that should not be the case. I tell clients when I speak that "Everyone is not your client." You may desire to serve the world and want everyone to purchase your product or service, but they won't. Think about it, what do you think about Wal-Mart and Target, Lays and Ruffles, the different types of Doritos and everyone does not purchase them nor like all of them, so what is going to set you apart from all of the others to ensure that you would be successful in your own business?

The most important thing is how you view yourself and what really resonates with you and your spirit along with how you do what you do. What you place out in the world as your Personal Brand is how you will be perceived and what others would say about you. What they think matters just as much as what you communicate to them. It is very important that you watch how you brand yourself because it is so hard to build a standing and everlasting brand, but it can turn around at any given point and go sour with one little minor thing. Building a brand should be explored more than just deciding what colors of a logo and what the copy-write says about you. When building your brand, it takes time, patience, consistency, attention and love for what you do and how you want to be viewed.

I have worked with clients who did not believe in themselves and I had more belief in them than they did in themselves. Your thoughts, energy and personality come through you as your brand. It is imperative that one must understand how you view yourself and how you position yourself is how your market will perceive you as well. As an authentic marketer, your brand should be a representation of you and your energy, which as you build a brand is based on what is in the inside, should be exuded on the outside. Therefore, your inner self is intertwined within

60   Elyshia Brooks.com

your brand. This is one way of staying unique from your competition because it is exactly what you bring to your business. It is the relationship that you are having with yourself that oozes into your business and how you do business.

As you walk out your true passion and purpose for your business, it becomes an intention that is birthed from the same place, which is as deep in your soul and heart for what you do. That place shares the same spirit, desire and attraction that will keep you moving forward and the capacity to articulate your brilliance as it relates to your expertise and specialty. As your business begins to align itself to attract and exist in the same space, you will begin to grow and be in sync totally with your divine clients. In other words, you are your business and you were designed for it; therefore, your brand, message and soul-filled purpose have a true meaning. When you give birth to what lies within, it begins to increasingly pull and push at the approach, service and product offered, and the message in which it is delivered. This is what is meant by soul-filled and heart-centered business because it has true meaning of purpose and good for those that it serves.

End of Chapter "Points to Ponder"

1. You have a gift, talent, or desire to serve others, so what good do you want to bring into the world with your business?

2. When you are serving in your heart-centered business, what brings you the most joy and satisfaction?

3. Your authentic marketing message is unique to you, so what is the message that you want to get out into the universe about how you want to serve your divine clients?

4. Your message should be clear and concise.

5. Become totally clear on your story how you will share with the world exactly who you are.

Chapter 4 – The Power of Authentic Marketing Attraction™?

KEY CHAPTER TOPICS COVERED

- Understanding What Authentic Client Attraction Is
- The Power of AMA
- How To Implement AMA

Authentic Marketing Attraction™ - What Is It?

Authentic *Marketing Attraction*™ is the most pure and simplest manner of sharing who you are with your ideal clients and they actually connect with you and know exactly what your soul speaks through your business. When you are using the *Authentic Marketing Attraction*™ process, you are really being as real as you possibly can and you share your gifts, talents and expertise with your divine clients. You are sharing a part of yourself from the deepest part of your soul with the world. The attraction is when the business aligns itself up with your purpose, guidance and energy that

We must have dreams if we are ever going to go anywhere significant and make a difference.

support your true authentic self. When you are authentically doing business from your heart and soul, it shows and it attracts all of those who are called to work with you. As you walk out your purpose in your business, you begin to transform your thinking to genuinely serving your divine right clients. You are excited to be walking in your calling or destiny.

Let's understand that marketing is all about marketing "you" and then your business if you are building a personal brand. You are your business; therefore, you need to have the right energy level and you have to produce consistent results because that speaks for you and your brand. *Authentic Marketing Attraction*™ draws to you who you really are and you are able to work with your divine clients which you enjoy working with you and you with them. Your energy sets the tone for your marketing and what it speaks for you.

65

Ultimately, as a conscious business owner, one has the meaning to create an energy that speaks to others right where they are and assist them in their playing BIG. As entrepreneurs expand their wings to walk out their destiny, it can be a little scary to create a brand and a marketing message that speaks to the world exactly who you are and what you offer. When starting a business, we all have butterflies and times when you wonder 'am I competent enough?' Or shall I say? I had these feelings and so have many of the clients that I worked with, because you want to share your talent and expertise. However, when in business one should be who they are and that includes understanding and operating in your true authenticity. As you walk out in the business world as an entrepreneur, you don't know everything, but you know what you know and are called to walk out, so knowing the difference between marketing and authentic marketing is imperative. Marketing, as we all may have known it to be, a collection of processes and channels that is designed to communicate and deliver value to customers in the form of a product or service. Yet, it sounds so simple but it actually stumps a lot of business owners because they don't understand it nor do they know the meaningful strategies that would work with their specific business.

As business owners come from or evolve into their authenticity, they are centered in who they are and the expertise that they bring to the world along with the value that is incorporated to create a brand which makes them different. Authentic Marketing looks at the value that one brings in business to its ideal clients because it represents your personal moral foundation and how you show up in your business daily. This could mean that you are bringing joy, gratitude, uniqueness, simplicity, and creditability to your business and these are the things that set you apart. You demonstrate your marketing message through the entire client experience from the time they come into contact with your message to the follow-up of the experience. In other words, it is not just transaction based but it is when you are conscious of your message and brand that you want them to have a memorable experience as they interact with you. Your business brand is really what makes others recognize who you are and what you bring and sets you apart from the others.

When you use the *Authentic Marketing Attraction*™ process in your business, there are a few questions that you must ask yourself when designing your business model and that is:

- How does your business speak and align itself with your authentic values, morals, purpose and passions?

- How does my authentic marketing voice speak to my divine clients and attract them to me while establishing a win-win business relationship?

- Have I become really clear on my core marketing message and brand that it represents; resonates, and is recognizable to my clients?

- Does my authentic marketing message, brand, communication style and business model have a concise and vibrant match that is spoken across the board?

- Do you have and know as much information about your divine client that you know their pain body and what keeps them up at night to their buying habits?

All of these questions mean something to your business' bottom line and ultimately creates an energy that embraces your ideal client's. As you become more and more clear about your ideal client's needs you are right on target with building an authentic marketing voice. Because you know who you are and you are walking in your authentic self, you begin to build your brand that truly brings value, a personalized awareness that resonates and creates a space that allows your clients to do the same. When your client works with you, they just "get you" and makes the relationship easier. Those who would benefit from Authentic Marketing would be those who really have a heart-centered and soul-centered business because those who are in business understand how it is about serving others. When a business incorporates authentic marketing strategies in their business model, it becomes more of a soulful connection that just works and feels genuine.

Why Authentic Marketing is Important to Growing Your Business

When growing your business even organically, you must understand that it will take time and nothing happens overnight. Success like that comes and it could happen to you, but when and if it does you must be prepared for it in order to be successful. When you are truly authentic in your business and others actually get what you are saying and know what you are doing in your business, then they can appreciate you more and give you more respect. Your authentic self would be the real you that your clients connect with and will build a relationship with. People connect people who are real and understand what they are dealing with and not someone who will talk down to them. Now with the social media it is easier to build genuine relationships with potential divine clients and strategic alliance partners.

As you build your brand for you and your business, it is important to know that you cannot service everyone and everyone is not your client. When you authentically build your brand and market your business it speaks directly to the client base that you need to speak to. Realistically, they will gravitate towards you. You cannot be afraid to turn away business because there are those who will waste your time and as you walk in your truthfulness, you have to be true to yourself. When you are being true to yourself, you know that "you cannot be all things to all people." You should only be working with that who are your divine clients and that is what Authentic Marketing Attraction is all about. You attract and work with your ideal clients as you walk in your authenticity.

Authentic Marketing Attraction™ is not only working with your ideal clients but having the power of understanding that the clients that you have are the exact ones that you are supposed to be serving. It is your truth and they connect to your truth both personally and professionally. It may take time to grow your business organically and

> *Change your focus, from making money to serving people. Serving MORE people makes the money come. – Robert Kiyosaki*

authentically, but it would be worth it because you are able to do your best work for them and the relationship is a win-win for both parties. You would enjoy the work and would be excited to do what you love. It becomes fun, so if it takes time to grow, at least it will be on your terms and you are living your dream. When one of my clients who was in the finance industry for majority of her life and then she discovered that she absolutely loved health and wellness and that is what kept her attention so she started a business doing just that. Now she is living her dreams everyday sharing with others about her passion and gift.

She knew exactly what she wanted to do, but could not get her marketing message clear enough to attract her divine clients, but she knew what her ideal clients looked like and exactly all that she needed to know to build a strong business. She eventually quit her job because she knew that she had to walk in her authenticity and she would turn clients down if they did not fit her ideal client profile because she knew that when she worked with those clients, she is her happiest, she is able to do her best work, and she knew the client would be excited to do the work. She understood that walking in her authenticity, she would be successful and she never looked back. Now her company is a six-figure business within one year. Because she got very clear on what her business, brand and path looked like and how she wanted to deliver to her divine clients consistently. She gets excited until this day because she wakes up and able to do her best at her passion. She went after her dreams and did not allow herself and other situations to hold her back. She never looked back. What does that look like for you?

Do you walk in your truth and authenticity every day? Do you absolutely know that you are walking in your gifts and talents, living your dreams? I ask this because so many people live the dreams and desires of others such as your parents and be who others want you to be. If that is the case you are not living authentically. Your business should represent who you are and what you were born to do. You may wonder how this may matter to your authentic marketing message, but it does and I am glad that you asked. When you are walking your truth, you are living your story and how you want to present yourself within your business is intertwined as well. It actually becomes a part of your life and how you live your life displays itself through your business. You cannot separate who you are in your personal life and your business if you are building a personal brand because it is all one together. All of which is to give you purpose and reason to live your dreams and the lifestyle that you desire even more.

How you grow your business depends totally on you and how you chose to build yourself. You can only grow, attract, and build as far as you are ready to receive. If you are not totally ready to grow your business and take it to the next level you will put out into the universe that you are not ready and that is what you will receive. So yes it does play a large role in what path you will design for yourself and your business. You must understand the purpose of a thing otherwise you will abuse and misrepresent it and that is not who you are. You don't want to misrepresent your business and who you are. You can only be true to self. Your life depends on you and that includes your business so you cannot let that part of you go when you are operating in your business. Your business is your God plan and how you chose to build and grow it depends on you being true to who are in and the business relationships that you engage in.

Does It Really Work and How?
How Is Authentic Marketing Used in Attracting Your Ideal Clients?

Authentic Marketing is in its purest form when you have a product or service that just needs to be, can be and would and could be purchased by a specific customer. When you are marketing authentically you are not offering gimmicks, tricks, or false tactics to get potential clients to purchase. When you are working from a space of authenticity, you are coming from a place of openness and integrity that grabs the heart strings of your potential divine clients. It is also based on building relationships that last and bring about brand loyalty. It is a radical approach that can evolve into a great authentic relationship building business model as opposed to a transactional relationship. Both the buyer and the seller agree that there is a mutual satisfaction that can interconnect other possible relationships. It is about building a marketing campaign around building relationships that are based on trust; which we have already heard that 'people do business with people they know, like and trust.' Without the trust factor and they like you based on exactly who you are and not the false pretense of what you could be.

When you are authentic in your marketing, you will get to know and understand your clients and they will get to know you in the same manner. After all, you are building a brand and a campaign that speaks to your exact client and you know how they think, purchase, behaviors, wants, desires and what their likes and dislikes are because you have done the research. When you are authentically attracting your ideal divine client, you are creating a 'customer experience' that would hold a favorable impression in their minds that will spark a relationship for brand loyalty. There are so many variables that contribute to developing a model that is comprehensible, duplicable, and encapsulates the business model and remain totally authentic in the process. The initial development of your business model should reflect this from the beginning because that is how you want to remain. There are many businesses that start out one way in their brand position and then change in midstream and it confuses the clients; which places in their mind 'can they be trusted to do what they say they would?' You must stay consistent.

Now that technology has changed the way customers make decisions and purchase, it has become an even greater challenge for business owners and marketers to obtain and retain them. So would you think that if you used all of the gimmicks and false tactics among all of the marketing clutter that they are bombarded with that they would remain loyal? Research states that customers receive about 30,000 impressions a day which includes, but not limited to, billboards, TV, radio, ads on apps on their cell phones and not to mention the Internet and so much more. What really makes you stand out from all of the rest especially if you are just getting started or rebranding? In other words, just look at the simple or complex concepts that you developing and how the customer would perceive you as either authentic or just like the rest of them all and perhaps puts you back in the midst of all the others only to be lost. You want to bring value to them and let them feel the total experience.

A suggestion could be to begin with is asking you "What does authenticity look like for me and my business and how my clients would view it?" If you would begin there, that would be a start. As you become more aware of whom you are and how you want to build your brand, you must do a few things that would keep you grounded in your authenticity. You would want to design a holistic approach to what you will demonstrate and to be the foundation of the brand and marketing message. First you have to do some soul-searching that would include getting clear with what your purpose and passion is behind your decision to build an authentic personal brand.

1. **Authentic Marketing & Branding Message** - what is the true message that you want to get out into the world that they would

know exactly what you are and what you stand for from a holistic approach. It is your uniqueness and value to your clients that you are here to serve.

2. **Authentic Purpose Statement** - This is a personal statement that you would hold to be true regardless of how the business grows. It is your foundational message that is the reason why you do what you do. It is your Value Proposition that you purposed your life and business to serve the world.

3. **Authentic Marketing & Branding Model** - it is your holistic and organic process that runs your business. It includes your foundation, systems and processes that take your clients through from start to finish creating that ultimate red carpet customer experience.

4. **Tell Your Story** – because people connect with stories and relate personally on some level. You are human and if you keep your experience to yourself, you cannot help others. Your divine clients need what is inside of you so share it.

5. **Ignite and Intertwine Your Passion** – with your skills, talents and experiences to attract your divine clients and do your best work. Your passion fuels you to think, grow and live BIG!

6. **Know Who You Are** – meaning your purpose, values, plans, desires, goals, strengths, weaknesses and aspirations. All of which makes up who you are so know yourself intimately so that you know how to bond with others.

7. **Develop Your Unique Promise** – which you want to commit to and be known for. When your divine clients look you up, what are they searching based on your promise and brand commitment? It should be obvious to you and them.

8. **Build Your Brand Bio** – that speaks all about you, what you offer and how you will provide a solution to their challenges. Your brand bio will enhance your virtual brand and attract others to you because it shares who you are and how you plan to communicate who you are.

9. **What is Your Social Cause** – or role that you stand in? What associations, organizations, causes or platforms that you and your brand can stand with? It should be something that you are drawn to and that you have a strong passion around and a personal connection to it.

10. **Purpose Your Brand** – with authenticity, relevance, engagement, unique, memorable and definitive in what it stands for.

When you incorporate all of this into your authentic marketing attraction process, you are able to attract those ideal clients that bring you great joy and much reward. It is your framework that identifies who you are in a world of so many different businesses. So flushing out this process should be the first things for your marketing concept. I have seen in many cases that many business owners just think of an idea on how to make money but don't consider the message they would like to put out into the world and they begin attracting the clients they don't want to work with and they find it so draining they quit doing what they thought would be a success. This process is not an easy one because it has to have meaning and some depth to it besides putting together a logo, website and getting some business cards. Your brand is your entire message to the world and how you plan to play BIG in the game. It has to be done organically and with a lot of attention and dedication.

The Power of Intentional Attraction in Marketing

Your thoughts, backed with energy, passion, faith and strong belief, is what you will need to attract your divine clients to you and your business. We have all heard of the Law of Attraction and how it lends itself to personal things, but it does have a place in business and marketing as well. We all go into business wanting so succeed and have abundance of clients, money, influence and respect; however, you should have an understanding that it is all reflective of your thoughts and actions. Who are you attracting? Where and how do you connect with them? What do they look like and are they willing to pay you what you are worth? It goes back to your thoughts. Case in point, when I first started my business, I was excited when new clients signed my contract and gave me that $100 deposit. But when I began to work with them, I began to feel a sense of drain and unworthiness because I felt that they did not respect the excellent work and service that I know to be very valuable. I knew what I offered was of great value to their business and ultimate success, but they did not value it, because they could not see it. So one day I was talking with my business coach and he says what is your deposit and sales process? I proceeded to share with him what that was and he said to me,

"You are afraid to discuss money and that is holding you back and you are attracting those clients who don't value your work. So I suggest that you increase your deposit to $500 and if you cannot discuss your pricing, then make a sales sheet and put it out on the website and they will know exactly what you offer and the value of it. Stop blocking your blessings with your thoughts and attracting those clients and watch your business grow."

Can you imagine what that meant to me at that point and how that changed my business and how I viewed myself and the value of my business? At that time, I was taken back because I was not ready to hear it, but it resonated with my soul and I changed the way I valued me and what I offered to the world. I too, consciously had to look inside and draw to me and my business that I wanted to work with and watched how those business relationships would begin to grow. What have you been attracting to you and what is holding you back from your greatness in your business?

You must become intentional in attracting to you and your business those clients that will build your brand and promise. You have the power to create a business you desire and to work with the clients who value your worth. You attract your divine clients that you love to work with and they love working with you because you are divinely walking your particular path and your brand is organically solid. How do you do attract them? Nonetheless, it does take you doing the inner work by knowing who you are and then the outer work, which is the planning and action behind the passion to build your brand. It does not just happen overnight for most, so you have to know you and the purpose of your brand. The power you have within you is specifically for you to serve and what you do with it depends totally on you. It is your divine birth right to be powerful in all that you desire to do and to have. You must be conscious and very intentional about what you want and how to connect your thoughts with how you see and view your business..

There is power behind being your authentic self because you can either contribute to the light of the world as you are walking in your truth the way only you can do it. So you do know the world is waiting for you to show up, stand up and PLAY BIG! They are waiting for your light to shine and for you to wake up to your original potential in serving in your business. The information you have and the business you operate need to come through you. It is time to "be" your authentic self, build an authentic brand and business that screams to the world your Extraordinary Passion because only you can do it like you can. Isn't time? So look at some action steps that would get you there.

LAW OF AUTHENTIC MARKETING ATTRACTION
TAKE ACTION LIST

- Envision your business success daily
- Sit and meditate on your divine clients...attracting them to you
- Believe in yourself and your dreams
- Create a vision board for your business...DREAM BIG!
- Journal your success daily
- Be grateful for your clients, expertise, business acumen, etc.
- Verbalize your desires daily
- Be totally passionate and sold out for your dreams
- Be joyful and happy
- Only work with clients that bring you joy
- Get comfortable talking about your worth and getting paid
- Think and focus only on the positive
- Your inner voice is KEY...Listen To It!
- Operate your business with confidence
- Trust in God, yourself and your dreams
- Get to know yourself inside and out
- Look for the best in every situation
- Give yourself away by being generous
- You must be willing to take risks and ACT!
- Love yourself and be honest to you and others
- Live your dreams daily!
- NEVER GIVE UP!!!

End of Chapter "Points to Ponder"

1. What Am I doing in my marketing that is attracting my divine clients?

2. What are my client's needs and challenges that I can provide a solution to base on my expertise and have significant results?

3. How can I serve my divine clients that would attract them to me?

4. How am attracting my divine clients? Where do I find them and how do I reach them? What is the best marketing channel?

5. Who do I intentionally want to attract in my business?

6. What are the clients that are going to bring me the most joy in working with?

Chapter 5 – Getting Clear About Your Authentic Marketing Message

KEY CHAPTER TOPICS COVERED

- Developing and Designing Your Authentic Marketing Message
- Understanding What Resonates With Your Spirit
- Attracting Exactly What You Want Through Your Message

What Resonates With Your Inner Spirit so That You Can Serve the World?

What do you want the world to know about what you do and how you serve? What is your authentic value proposition (AVP) that you offer consistently? What do you want your divine clients to know about you so that it resonates with them so they are propelled to call and inquire to work with you? Your inner spirit should be at peace with your relation to serve them wholeheartedly; therefore, your marketing message should reflect as such. As you brand and design an authentic marketing message that speaks to your clients, there are a few things you must look at and answer for yourself. It is not always easy to design unless you are totally in-tuned and tapped into your being or soul so you know how you can attract and grow your business. But you know what is in your heart and spirit but you don't know how to design a message that can be translated into your marketing and branding. Let's dive into it.

Your spirit or soul is your inner-being, inner-knowing which allows you to just "Be." It is where everything begins and ends as it keeps you focused on your purpose and passion. It is your gifts, talents, anointing, or calling; whatever, you want to call it that speaks to you as it creates the divine desire to live out your purpose. It is your higher being that settles in you and creates a foundation for which you are to design a marketing message for that purposeful business. It has meaning and growth behind all that you do. Everything does not resonate with your spirit so you know that you have to take time to get connected or plugged into a Higher Power, that of spirit or energy, if you chose to believe or not to believe. It is how you set a foundation for your business visualization and models that are to follow. Your business is built on solid values that share and connect with you on a higher level.

What You See is What You Authentically Receive?

When we know within ourselves that someone is not being sincere nor authentic do we begin to feel it from their energy that is given off. How does that make you feel? What does that say to you in terms of how you will respond or react? When we feel that someone is not being genuine, it tends to say that, this person does not value me enough to be truthful and authentic. Then there is the feeling that they are not because they are feeling they are not good enough to be in your presence and needs to pretend or non-authentic.

As one grows and evolves with their business, there is a time when you know that what you put out there is what you will receive back to you. Therefore, knowing and really paying attention to what you put out into the

> *What you put out there, is what you will ultimately receive.*

world is what you will receive more of. If you want more clients that want and need exactly what you offer, you begin to attract who you want to work with, then the more they will come. How you attract your divine clients totally depends on you and what you put out into the universe and have faith to believe. You are the mirror in which you see yourself as the owner of your business, CEO or president of your idea and you know who you want to work with and how you can do your best work. No one knows how you can do it your way but you, so why not work with your clients that bring you the most joy because you are giving your energy, knowledge and time away. Your passion should speak to every fiber of your being with the most positive energy and so you can attract that back to you just the way that you envision it. You are the creator of your business enterprise and knowing this is the beginning of how you will build your authentic marketing message.

Also, what you believe about you and your business plays a huge role in your marketing message because it has a force of energy behind it. Think of this; you are sending off negative thoughts about lack and there are not enough clients out there that will sustain your business and live the lifestyle that you desire, so your entire energy that you send out comes back to you. If your marketing message sends out vibes that you need clients and you are sounding desperate, then your potential clients will receive it as such and people

You will succeed in anything if success is never defined; however, success is definable and attainable.

resonate and do business with whom they are attracted to. It is the ultimately the message that you send out which creates and open vibrant space or a closed space of lack. Honestly, your divine clients can sense your energy and you don't want to send out energy of lack and desperation because you have to stay true to your business model and your brand promise. Compromising your brand promise and integrity will have serious consequences especially when you are building an authentic conscious-centered personal brand. As you begin to change your mind set on your marketing, authentic personal brand and your message, it becomes imperative that you stay true to your values and purpose. What type of energy are you sending out now? What do you want to attract you and your business? It is up to you!

How to Say What You Need To Say

When you have to say something really important, how do you communicate it to others where it will grab their attention and hold it while understanding completely? When you communicate your services and products to your ideal clients, do they catch it the first time and do they get exactly what you do the first time? Knowing what to say, when to say it and the intentions on what you want to say all depends on your purpose behind what you want to do. As a business owner you must be willing to share with the world which who you are and how you communicate it to them and how they receive it is important. There are several components that should be included in the communication process with the understanding that what is said and how it is said is very important. It first starts with knowing who your ideal clients are and what their needs would be so that you can speak directly to it.

- The communication should be receptive in a manner that could change and have an effect in favor of the client to solve a problem.
- The social context, groups of reference and the influence should be powerful enough to get them to take action for their own purpose.
- The effect is much higher when the message is clear and in line with what the receiver needs to hear at any particular time.
- The message that is communicated should be one that connects with the divine client's value system and resonates in their spirit.

Now in the new economy, the client has a lot more to filter and control over what they would like to receive and through what channel. They have become higher in involvement in how they interact with various brands too. It is really up to the business owner to become really

85

in-tuned with how their divine clients receive their marketing message. Therefore, the message should share some:

- **Awareness** - the client has to become aware of the brand and there must be a way for the knowledge to be deciphered and filtered so that an educated decision can be made. If the knowledge in the message is weak and cannot be understood, the client will be challenged in receiving it and the closing of the sale could be lost. The client should be made aware of the products and services that are available after being inundated with the possibilities of what you are offering.

- **Appreciation** - Once the clients are aware of your product or service, they would develop an appreciation of it and they begin to feel a certain way about it because it triggers something in them that speaks to them and what they need solved.

- **Predilection** - As the client builds and emotion around their preference which may or may not be preferred to others perhaps by the features, benefits, and maybe the performance that is provided.

- **Persuasion** - Because there are so many products and services available, the persuasion may not be strong enough for the client to work with you and purchase your products. The conviction has to be one of interest in order to move a client to purchase, but it must remain true at all times because your clients can tell if you are not.

- **Investment** - The message should be communicated in such a way that the consumer will invest in your offer. However, the investment can be immediate or it can be drawn out to the where the client will need to think about the investment. This has a lot to do with price, the message that was delivered, premium offerings, less expensive offerings and such. The investment is the important part of the process because it is the ultimate goal of.

How you communicate your message from the above should be considered so that your marketing message has direction and clarity on what your intended goal shall be. It can be a challenge if you are totally clear on what you want to communicate to the world about what you do. Your intentions should be simplistic so that there is no real confusion about your offerings. Your divine clients will not invest, if the message is not clear and the communication is processed the way that you intended.

Creating Your Authentic Voice

Your "*Authentic Voice*" is who you are to the very core of your being and it speaks to the business that you operate, the clients that you serve, the message that you send out and the results and solutions that you provide. Your voice is AMAZING to you and for you, because when you speak to the world you know exactly what you were called to do and how to serve. Your voice speaks volumes on how you create a business that is centered around your purpose and passion as it becomes intertwined in all of your marketing collateral, branding and messaging. There are several steps in creating your "authentic voice" so that it is received in such a manner that shares your genuine self. It is the truth of who you are and the essence of your being so how you communicate that depends on how you are able to connect emotionally with your divine clients.

Step 1: What do you want to share with the world about who you are?

Step 2: What presence do you want to have when you command the room?

Step 3: What is your soul telling you about you and your purpose?

Step 4: What are you passionate about that burns deep in your soul?

Step 5: What are you pursuing, mastering and redefining?

Step 6: What are your processes and systems to live and do business authentically?

You must know the answers to these questions because that is the truth of you and the essence of your business. You need to know it in such an intimate way that only you can know.

To create an "Authentic Voice and Message" you would need to first understand and become more aware of who you are and what business you were born to do and then develop processes and systems that would help you to pursue what you desire. It is about what feels right to you and not anyone else. Once you know this, you will begin only attracting and pursing clients that brings you the greatest joy and satisfaction. Instead of spending so much money in marketing that is not attracting your divine clients, you begin to do what it takes to get true clarity on who they are and exactly where to find them because you all will be on the same pathway and spirit connects with spirit; just as like attracts like. This will take out the guesswork and show you if you are wasting your time and money on those who are not attracted to your soul work. You are not playing the traditional marketing game that is either hit or miss, manipulative and condescending. That is not who you want to attract because you won't be able to receive the joy from your soul work.

Your soul work will allow you to create environments that would support your authentic marketing and branding lifestyle and not the manipulative marketing tactics that get you the wrong clients. You are focusing on the purpose, passion and the effortless abundance that you are attracting because that is where your soul is. It is in a place of abundance, supporting others and being totally who you are in your business and personal life that creates an authentic branding lifestyle. You are one with your business and who you are.

End of Chapter "Points to Ponder"

1. What is the message that you have to share with the world?

2. What speaks directly to who you are and who you want to serve?

3. What character traits do you want to be known for?

4. What is the marketing lifestyle that you see yourself living and can live up to in both your business and life?

5. What is the best way for you to communicate and then communicate the way that you are most comfortable with?

Chapter 6 – Attraction of Divine Client Relationships

Key Chapter Topics Covered

- What Are Divine Clients?

- How To Build A Divine Business Relationship

- Win-Win Strategies For Attracting Divine Clients

What Are Divine Client Relationships?

Now that you are totally clear on your purpose, passion, calling, gifts or anointing; you can begin to look at exactly who you come here to the earth to serve. You have clarity on who you are and what your message should be saying about what you do and how you should serve in your business. As you evolve, your business and the world around you evolves and you are always in a constant state of moving and being that you in connection with others all of the time and any given moment. You are a human being making choices in moments to serve others and how you do serve is up to you. However, now that you have some clarity around all of what you did not know about yourself, it is time to look at who you are here to serve.

A "Divine Client" is one who others call the ideal client, niche, or target market. But you *Go within your soul to find your purpose and passion.* Divine Client is one who you know, claim and love working with. They are the individuals who resonate and are called to work or purchase something from you and the connection is there where the ultimate relationship is formed. It is as if your spirits are connected and you both come together to serve the world in a bigger way in terms of you serving your divine client and they are getting what they need to serve the world in a bigger way as well. So together you are both serving in a manner that is true to whom you are and you are walking in your purpose together. The connection is greater than you can imagine because the spirit between the two are of the coming together to participate in a movement of some sort.

I truly believe that when you are working with your divine clients you are serving your best because they are an extension of who you are. So when you can build your business around your divine clients, you are making what you enjoy more exciting and you are making more connections. That is when you know that you are walking in your purpose and serving who you are supposed to serve. When you are thinking about whom

Your divine clients wake you up daily with absolute joy!

you would like to serve, you must get very clear and understand who they are and become really serious about connecting with them as you would about your friends. Your clients do represent you and your best work; therefore, you must know them. When I say they represent you, they are participating in building your brand and the kind of work that you do, will reflect in your happy clients and you doing your best work.

Your divine clients are those with whom you are waking up to every day to work because you get them and they get you while paying you what you are worth. How exciting is that? Once you know who they are, you can see that when you come in contact with someone who is not your divine client it will become apparent. You will feel some resistance to your spirit and showing up and doing your best work will become a chore. I have had that experience more often than I care to share, but I can tell you every time that I did, it became where I did not want to do the work. I would put it off for as long as I could. I then had to make myself do the work and to decide that when I feel this way about a client, I must be true to myself and decline the client; perhaps refer them to a business partner. It was much easier to do that than to vex my spirit unnecessarily when I have a choice that I can make. I had to own it and honor how I was feeling because I am committed to do my best work and nothing less.

As you become more aware and in tuned with who you are supposed to serve, it will become much easier to recognize. When a non-divine client begins to work with you, you will see how they drain and zap your energy. It begins to frustrate you which does not allow you to show up and be your best self. Then you may say, 'Well, I need the money.' Really, of course you go into business to make money but I truly believe that "Every dollar is NOT my dollar" because I have come to a place where I am just committed to my happiness and me. For me, that is showing up and showing out on what I just love to do and to compromise that would do nothing for me but make me doubt my commitment to myself, business, brand and then it takes me away from doing my best work for those clients that I adore working with. In business that is soul-full and heart-centered you must become open and honest with yourself on exactly what that looks like and how that makes you feel.

How to Build an Authentic Divine Relationship

Authentic Divine Relationships are those that are built on true, open and honest commitment that seeks to become a relationship that should and could be long-term. The relationship is founded on a firm foundation that includes sincerity, trust that can be mutually valuable. These relationships last much longer after the transaction is complete. Relationships are very important in business. With all of the available social media reaching, building and enhancing the relationship is vital to the sustainability of growth and profits. In other words, businesses cannot afford to build strong authentic and divine relationships simply to build their brand loyalty. Businesses are recognizing that some if not most of their marketing efforts should be geared towards authentic and divine relationships because they believe in their product or service.

As companies have changed a moderate part of their marketing strategies to include authentic relationships, it has become apparent to many that it is crucial not to include because of the competition is very strong. Look at the Apple business, it has not only snagged three-fourths of the technology market, but have made a great effort to sell their products. As we see when we frequent the Apple store, they have built a team of knowledgeable employees that seek to build relationships around their products, hoping to get them back in the store. The relationship in the store may be short but as long as the products are of quality and they stand behind their brand, the long-term relationships will continue to last. Steve Jobs knew that the product would sky-rocket and he built an empire with customer service and relationships.

The world stands aside to let anyone pass who knows where they are going. –
David Starr Gordon

It has been reported that it costs 7-8 times or more to obtain a new customer as opposed to retaining the customer. Additionally, a business or organization could possibly lose about 50% of their client base from the previous five years. That timeframe is possibly a little shorter with the capabilities of social media. Studies show that with customers receiving multiple ads throughout the day, it can be even harder to keep them loyal. Therefore, building authentic divine relationships that actually last is a win-win of value for all parties involved. In today's world, it takes a little more effort to catch the attention of your divine client unless you are totally clear on how they think, where they hang out, who they do business with. Are they at networking events, participating in certain online communities or are they attending conferences and trade shows? You must know how to reach them and attract them.

Building Divine Client Relationships to Grow Your Business to Millions

When you are working with your divine clients, you are able to do your best work and they are able to pay you what you are worth because they are committed to what is inside of you. You attract them based on what is in your soul and what you believe that you know that you came to the earth to do. There are divine clients out there that are meant only to work with you; therefore, you must reach them right where they are. Where they are can be many places so marketing in one way is not beneficial for you and your business. You must research them; know where they frequent, how they buy, what they are buying and what the value they are looking for is. You have to be your authentic self because that's who they trust you to be when you do meet them either via teleseminars, conferences or at speaking engagements. You must do the work for them to see, feel, and to quantify what you offer and the value that it brings to them.

First when you are you are looking for your divine clients, you must have total clarity in who you can do your best work with based on

Self-trust is the first secret to success.

97

what brings you joy, serves them in a positive win-win manner and adds value to them holistically. Your divine clients are looking for exactly what is inside you and will connect with that and pay you what you are worth. Your values, morals, and your soulful work is what open the doors to attracting exactly who you need to work with. So let's look at some ways to attract divine clients that can help you grow your business to millions if that is your desire.

1. List your divine client types based on the services and products that you offer. You must do this based on every product and service that you offer because each speaks to a different audience.

2. Know their demographics. Your divine clients are not all in one place, so expand your thoughts and think big because if you don't you will remain small because of your thinking. (Ex. Gender, age, occupation, income, education, marital status, location, race, ethnicity, etc.)

3. Know what you are comfortable with in terms of your marketing channels. I say this because some are not good at making calls but rather email marketing. You must know what your strengths and weaknesses are so you are not spinning your wheels and wasting valuable time.

4. Know both your primary and secondary divine clients. These will both generate clients and build your list, which results in higher profits. Primary clients are those that you speak directly to in the core of your business. These are the ones that the majority of your marketing will attract. Secondary clients are those that are not your true divine clients but they resonate with you and will buy your

products because they had some connection or they will at some point.

5. Design a marketing campaign based on how your divine clients will receive and view them not how you want to give it. It must come from a place of serving and just getting more money.

6. Think of your markets as you design your programs and products with how will they purchase and what is the best way for them so that you don't lose your value.

7. Understand your divine client's psychographics and how they receive your marketing message. These are their behaviors, decision making skills, external and internal perceptions, gratification and what drives them.

8. Design your Purchasing Design Model that includes how your divine clients purchase and you closing the deal. In this model you are looking at their awareness of your brand, product acceptance, purchasing your offer and then how you will follow up with your customer service management.

9. Know your divine clients on an unconscious and conscious level. This is based on your associations, networks, and influences that would connect with them to purchase. In your marketing what would trigger them to buy based on an association with something else? For instance, like perfume with a particular outfit or model.

10. Know what is attracting your divine clients through value, performance, positioning, USP (Unique Selling Proposition), brand, commodity, and relation of the product or service as a whole.

Working on and thinking about these ten items, is crucial to developing a product or service that speaks directly to your divine clients. It is sure to give you some clarity that can bring in more clients for your business. However, you must get really clear on who you want to serve.

Knowing What to Say Authentically That Speaks to Your Divine Clients

Now that you know who your divine clients are, you must know what to say to attract them to you both consciously and unconsciously. They are attracted to what you put out into the universe and what speaks to them as to what you are offering. What the connection may become is an emotional response to what is relational to your offering. Since you have experienced and know what you have had to endure and you know what your expertise is you can speak confidently. Your confidence will pull at their heart strings, speaks to their soul or solves their pain body. Your message should be clear and understandable with the intentions pure and authentic.

Success is not perfection; success is slightly above average.

When you speak it should be intentional and grab their attention so that they are intrigued to want more information. Because you know that you can offer results, your message has to be clear on what you can provide for them and the value that will increase their probability.

The reason entrepreneurs are not attracting their divine clients is because they are not aware of what should be said and way to say it that is compelling, strong and has a call to action. You need to share with them your solutions, value, results, and benefits that will influence them in a positive manner to work or purchase from you. You have to become relational with them and meet them right where they are because if you don't establish a deeper connection than the surface transactional process, you are not guaranteed the repeat business or the referrals. Grabbing their attention is so important especially if you are building a business that is sustainable. It is really time out for transactional processes because with all of the social media avenues, it has become intentionally relational.

Knowing how to authentically speak to your divine clients takes a look at your personal soul and how you are created and wired to connect with others. It is a sacred time in which you are to get really still and see what that energy feels like. You will recognize the truth that is within your being and you get to the very core. You become quiet and centered on figuring out the why and not necessarily the how. You will directly be inspired to action that will align itself with you and your divine clients in such a way. It is when there is no resistance in how you connect *An unused life is an early death.* with your divine clients. Being should not be hard and when you communicate your messaging and language around what you do, it aligns itself with your divine clients that they will show up to support you because you are speaking their language. They will show up and connect with you on a deeper level and share it with others. It becomes more about your willingness to serve others that your message will give a higher energy.

Let's look at some tools to that will guide you in knowing exactly how to communicate your message to those you want to serve. It will take time for some but in order to live the peace, abundance and happiness to work with your divine clients, it takes work. Some may get it early and some may already know, and some have no clue right now but all of that is okay. I cannot stress enough that you must get totally true, centered, and obtain clarity in the process before you know that you can serve and who and why you are connected to those divine clients. First of all,

A. Get in a quiet place in an open position to receive.

B. Have a pen and pad with you so that you can write things down if your memory is challenged.

C. Ask the questions and feel the energy and the connection of what is deep in your soul.

D. Surrender and ask for assistance to know what you need to know to connect and receive.

Ask these questions:

1. Ask yourself what is the 'why" that I am seeking that my divine clients are seeking solutions to?

2. What do I need to be guided to in order to bring solutions, value and abundance to my divine clients?

3. What is it that resonates with me and what are my divine clients having a pain body with or in a struggle? How can I serve?

4. Know what the spirit and energy will guide so ask what that looks like for you.

Strategies That Create Win-Win Marketing For You and Your Clients

- As a professional entrepreneur, you must build your credibility and trustworthiness for you divine clients.

- Know that it is not all about the money but the experience that you create and the solutions that you provide. Money is important but you need to get clear on your relationship with money.

- Brand and market yourself and your business in a professional manner that will attract clients.

- Create avenues that open doors for you and others.

- Create an advisory board that can share your vision and can push you into your growth.

- Know exactly how you connect to your divine clients.

- Ask for what you really want and allow that process to unfold.

- Learn to speak from the heart and soul with a smile and be confident in who you are and what you offer.

- Learn to LISTEN! You must do this because it is what they are telling you that they need. You have to honor what they say so be truly present with all of your divine clients.

- Develop some standards of service of how you will serve your divine clients.

Knowing the Power Within to Capturing Your Authentic Clients that Enjoy Working with You and You With Them

When I discuss knowing the power within, that means doing the work to learn your soul language and how that resonates with your true being and the souls of your divine clients. It is harder to do if there is resistance to what you know to be true for yourself. As a business owner you have to believe that you are powerful and magnificent in what you do and there is a responsibility that comes with

> *Until you value yourself, you won't value your time. Until you value your time, you will not do anything with it.*
> *— M. Scott Peck*

that because you have to play and show up because your divine clients are waiting for you to do so. It is not too much work if you are shifting your mindset and looking within and not so much of looking out into the world. All that you need and what you have to offer is within you. Your bliss should be that you are serving others who absolutely love what you bring to their life and the quality of the relationship and what you give you receive back. The greatness is within you if you allow yourself to be guided by what is in your soul.

Your power within will connect with your clients because that is where they need to be. As you begin to walk in your purpose and knowing, you are walking in your divine state. With that you must begin to know yourself inside and out because as you learn more about you, you can connect with more clients and be who you are supposed to be. Your clients need you. They need what is inside of you and you are short-changing the world if you are not living up to your fullest potential. It is time to show up and play big in life. You cannot stay stuck in what you know that you should be doing. Stop shrinking back. Live the life and grow the business that you are divinely created for.

End of Chapter "Points to Ponder"

1. What is your spirit and soul telling you about serving your divine clients?

2. What are your strengths and weaknesses both interpersonally and in business?

3. What are you resisting that is keeping you from abundance in working with divine clients?

4. What is your communication style and how does it help or harm you in serving your divine clients?

5. Do you really know who you are, what you offer and why you are here to serve?

Chapter 7 – Pricing Your Value & Worth for the World You Serve

KEY CHAPTER TOPICS COVERED

- Know Your Business' Worth

- Understanding your Value and Pricing Accordingly

- Learning How To Ask For What You Deserve

Knowing Your Business' Worth

When you begin to think of your value and self-worth, can you put a dollar figure to it? Can you put a price to what you yourself have the knowledge of, the time and effort that you have put the energy into it? What do you offer to the world that is so valuable that there is no amount of money that can be paid for it? Your pricing speaks a great deal about how much you value your expertise and ability to provide a service or product. There are several motivations that can be achieved. As an authentic business owner, you should be very comfortable with what you charge because you must be compensated for what you are worth and nothing less. What is your motivation and how does it affect your bottom line. Ask yourself is the price too high? Too low? Or just right? Because you must understand that this is your hard work that you have studied and mastered so you must get real comfortable about discussing money.

This chapter discusses "Pricing." We cannot address pricing unless we address having a "Healthy Money Mindset" and an "Abundant Relationship" with Money because that is one of the biggest things that are holding us back as an entrepreneur and business owner. What one thinks and believes about money can either bring more to them or draw from them. I use to think that this is not true, but it really is true because if one comes from a place of lack and scarcity, they would eventually live in such a place constantly in their minds. How could one go any further if they are always thinking that there is not enough for everyone and always broke?

COMPLETE THOUGHTS AND FEELINGS ABOUT MONEY

I have some money mantras and affirmations that you can use to build your faith and soul around money, wealth and abundance further in the book. However, it would be good to design your own that you can relate to personally.

Build a Business Around Your Expertise and Stay in Your Lane

When you have experience, education, and expertise in your field of industry, you should know your stuff; which you know that you know because you can do it in your sleep. You can talk about it with anyone and you can speak about it to thousands. Your expertise is what you know inside and out. You are an expert in your area and it is okay if you are not as proficient in marketing, accounting or whatever it may be; and if that is the case, then it is time to get those around you that do. Your business is about how you serve your divine clients and you need all of the expertise around you so that you can serve to your highest good in your lane. If you don't know that you are out of your lane, your clients will sense it and recognize the energy that you give off and will cause the prospect to not purchase.

It is imperative that you are in complete and total alignment because what you do represents who you are and the brand that you are seeking to represent. When you are coming out of alignment, you will walk into another realm in which you are not comfortable, you would not want to do the work, in fact you will resist doing the work because that is not what satisfies you. You must be true to yourself and say to yourself, "I know that I am out of my element and that is not okay, because this is not the work that brings me joy and happiness." When you are walking in your true authentic purpose, it is not hard and if you have to struggle against something outside of your lane will cause doubt and heartache because you will work with a client that you are not divinely supposed to serve.

> *Plan purposefully, Prepare prayerfully,*
> *Proceed positively, Pursue persistently!*

This has happened to a client of mine who knew their calling is definitely strategy management, but because they were in a place of 'needing' money, they took clients on that were not in their primary market or niche and ended up getting sued because they went out of their element, expertise if you would, to do something such as accounting and lost all of the client's money. That valuable lesson shares a whole lot because it is a life and business lesson that is very valuable and one worth paying attention to.

> *Build your business based on your knowledge, expertise and experiences.*

Therefore, it is imperative that you do only what you are called to do, your expertise, emotional intelligence, and the alike will open doors for you. When you started your business, you knew exactly what your expertise and passion were and that is why you started, so if you have not developed some other skills, stay in your lane because you cannot be all things to all people. If you step out the lane, you will begin to see your primary divine clients become confused and you don't want to do that for them.

What is Your Value Worth?

What is your worth? What is so special about you and what value do you bring to serve your divine clients? What it the purpose of your worth? You need to know the answer to these questions because you have got to know so that others will know. You should know your own worth so others can see it as well, because you believe in you. See your value, put a cost to is and know what your expertise is. You know your material and how to share it because you can do it the way you know how to do it. Your value is determined by you and what you know that you can offer along with what it is that is demanded by your divine clients. Your value is what you know, who you know and how you serve. Your education, expertise, and experiences have brought you this far. You know what is already inside of you and what you have come to the earth to do. It is your divine purpose and truthfully there is no number that you can say you are because you are priceless. However, you can suggest a figure based on the going rates of the industry.

You have got to know your worth in order to bring forth the fruit of your purpose because the world is depending on you. Your value is joined together with your spirit and what comes from your spirit is what is priceless.

What are your top five values that you live by? Know them!

Worth means that there is something good or important enough to justify and having value of or equal in value to; therefore, in other words is your value just all about money? Your value has to be worth more than money itself. It must go deeper than that. I have worked with clients who have paid me in full cash for my services and did not do what they were committed to do. My family and friends say "Well you got paid for your services," which may be true but because I know my worth and my value that I bring to each and every client, I want to see the fruit of my value and worth come to fruition. That is what means more. I am not saying go out and start a business and work for free. What I am saying is you have got to have a heart to serve others rather than just be about the money. Your mission has to become deeper than the money that you make. Money is very important but it is not everything when you have a bigger passion, purpose and mission to serve, because the money will come, trust the process. You know that you want to see your value, gift and expertise manifested, which will bring a greater sense self-worth.

Design a price that is around what you know you are worth and how you consistently bring great results and solutions to your divine clients. As you grow your business, your significance and worth will continue to grow. You will know when and how to raise your prices and set according to what you believe and know what your worth is despite what others may be charging. Stay in your lane and grow at your own pace and will.

How to Ask for What You Deserve and No Less

First, you must have an irresistible offer, product or service that creates opportunities that will open the door for asking for what you deserve. The client would have to see the value and how it can truly serve them or provide a solution for them that is worth their investment. When you are pricing your services and products the return-of-investment (ROI) should be significant and about twenty to twenty-five percent above your fee. The key is knowing what your divine clients are willing to invest in and then also what the emotional connection between you and the client is. There needs to be an understanding of what they are willing to invest in, honor and also refer to others. If clients are coming to you it's because they have some kind of connection with you and they believe in you; therefore, asking for what you deserve should not be hard. I say it is not hard because you know that you are good at and have expertise in so; whatever, they trust you to bring it.

When I first started out, I was so reluctant to share what my prices were and was afraid to ask for what I deserved. But yet, I was complaining that I was not making what I am worth. Well, at that time, I was only charging a deposit of $100 when they signed my contract on services started at $800, yes see that right. I was not even getting half the deposit. At that time I was complaining to my Business Coach Andrew Morrison, who said look at the caliber of clients you are obtaining with your $100 deposit. These were clients who really did not honor nor value the services that I offered because I did not honor myself and my expertise. I was attracting those clients to me who were NOT my divine clients because I was so resistant to serving them. Andrew told me to raise my deposit to $500 and stick to it no matter what and that would weed out those who are not serious about doing business with me. I did and I did begin to get those who were more serious but that did not mean they would follow through on their commitment to do the work.

Now that my business has evolved into my true divine purpose, I have only committed myself to only working with my divine clients because they are the ones that I do my best work with and I am not doing the busy work that was just that…"busy"! You have to know what you want and do it to the best of your ability and then don't settle for nothing less because you know your worth. So now, what it is your worth and how do you get paid for it? Because it was initially hard for me to talk about my fees, my business coach suggested that I create a Rate Sheet on my website and carry one around with me and perhaps give it out when I gave my information. Whatever is your best way to communicate, that is good for you, do that. Either you can:

- Put it in your media kit along with other information such as brochures, press releases, etc.

- Add to your website

- Get comfortable and practice asking

The Power of Consistently Market to Your Ideal Clients That Yield Big Profits

Product Life Cycle

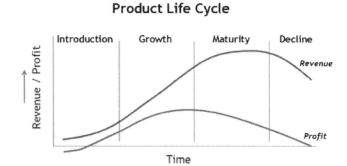

Introduction Phase

The Introduction Phase is the one of the most important aspects of the whole cycle because it will give you an opportunity meet new people and practice your people skills. You are aware of the sensitivities, competition, monopolies, attitudes and behaviors can be monitored and you are able to receive first-hand information on what others believe about your business and you are able to obtain understanding of your divine clients.

In this phase, you have to understand that there will be some that will not accept what you are offering and you should know that your product and service is not for "EVERYONE" so expect some pull-back and know that you are still in your right place. This phase a business owner will show you how much you believe in your own product or service because it will test you and your character and challenge you to doubt yourself, but you must keep the faith because you know that you know that you are meant to be serving in this capacity.

Introduce yourself, your brand, product and service to the world in which you are to serve and know that you are walking in your divine path and despite the opposition there are others who will believe and purchase your product service because your soul and spirit connects, which means you are supposed to work with each other. Do not become discouraged in this phase but understand that you will receive valuable information that you can use that can catapult your business into the next level. Do not give up in this phase.

Growth Phase

This phase is where you are have awareness and there is buzz around you and your business. This phase if the fun part because you are walking in your path and you are having fun doing what you set out to do and serve in a manner that is so rewarding. The Growth Phase is so exciting because you are in the right space mentally with your money marketing mindset and you are walking in abundance. Additionally, within this phase, you are noticing that your competition has become a little more noticeable and are sharing a lot of what you are seeking to do but know that your competition is just that those who are called to serve in a similar manner as you but not how you do and serve your clients. Your style, expertise, programs, communication methods, WOW Experience is totally different from what others offer. Please don't focus your attention on the competition but instead look at them as your motivators to stay on top of your game and explore ways of becoming a better you. You know that you were called to serve the way that you are. Don't sweat the small stuff but enjoy the growth because some of their clients may prefer working with you so allow it to play a bigger part in how you serve and not from a place of lack and scarcity.

Mature Phase

At this stage you have developed brand recognition, loyalty and equity that have shown to stand the test of time and your competitors have noticed are figuring out ways to become different and perhaps design a variation of what you are offering which then pushes you to create and design other much needed products. It is about how you relate your success to how other who wants to be like yours. It can be flattering but know that you are called with a purpose and you much keep moving forward with the understanding that if you did not have others to share in your passion, then you would not be on the pathway where you are supposed to be.

Decline Phase

In this stage you are looking at what needs to be phased out, changed and or even re-tweaked so that you can increase sales again. At some point this maybe when some of the competition has become stiff and has made the marketplace a little overflowed with the same information which at this point, you know what you need to do. It is time design a new service, product or program that speaks to another place where you divine clients may be at this time. It is all a part of the cycle to continue growing, changing, implementing and reassessing where you are in your business and where you want to go next.

I did not speak about the normal Product Life Cycle in terms of the traditional sense because we all get that, but there are a lot of my divine clients who struggle with all aspects of the cycle from a mindset change and what is inside needs to shift in order to keep moving in the direction that they are supposed to be going. Each phase is different and how you view it and look into it, makes for a way of life that you either want or don't want based on your mindset and how you receive what life shares with you through experiences.

Cost Pricing Techniques

Price = (Unit allocation to fixed costs + Unit Variable Cost) x (1 + percent markup)

EXAMPLE

Kreative Marketing Group, Inc. has placed a contract for a marketing advertising proposal. There are certain terms and price constrictions that would include salaries, R&D, insurance, design and cost producing variables. Under this proposal there is a guaranteed 25 percent profit to complete the project.

Unit Variable Cost = $20,000

Unit allocation to Fixed Cost = $15,000

Profit = 25 percent

Unit Price = ($20,000 + $15,000) x (1 + 0.25) = $31,250

As a business owner and entrepreneur, you should know what your costs are and where you stand at all times financially; perhaps even using a daily tally sheet to keep track of all your sales for each day is a suggestion. It is critical to know where your business finances are and what are the key determinants that make your business stable? What your hot sellers are? You should make effective pricing decisions about your financial strategies that will catapult you forward. Although, what I am about to say may be a little questionable but I feel that I need to say it. "You cannot be attached to the outcome of your finances." As a business owner it is possible for you to separate yourself from your business but not your brand. Financially speaking, you should know your financial value and know what is coming in and what is going out because you will need money to continue to fuel your business and grow your brand. It is truly suggested that you be involved in your financial picture but consciously become detached from the outcome.

> *There are no shortcuts to any place worth going. –*
> *Beverly Sills*

End of Chapter "Points to Ponder"

1. What is your worth and value?

2. What are your unit costs for each product, service, or program

3. Do you know your seasons of Growth and where you are in your business?

4. What is your preferred method of asking for what you are worth?

5. What is your expertise so that you don't go out of your lane?

Elyshia Brooks.com

Chapter 8 – What Makes Your Business Unique and Results Different?

Relationship Marketing Strategy

Over the years marketing and branding have changed and that is because the consumers have changed. In the early years, marketing was geared toward the masses. The thought was "If we make it then customers will purchase." Therefore, there was mass production of products but that became too expensive and wasteful because everyone did not like the same things, so then making customized products became the way to go. Then there was strategic planning

> *You are unique and what you bring to your business is unique!*

and designing, which is a process around the assets, functional areas, and other opportunities that to provide face-to-face marketing. We have seen the market go from consultative to transactional to strategic planning and now we are in the Relationship Strategy of marketing.

Relationship marketing now is about establishing relationships that are more focused and not pretentious about just a transaction. The relationships are more about what does the client want and need, then how to make the product or service to satisfy the client. When there is more focus on building a relationship that are truly authentic with the thought of actually creating an experience. Relationships are supposed to be nurtured and engaging and should be enhancing some characteristic that you come to that relationship to learn. When you are looking for a Unique Selling Proposition you may look at your Relationship Marketing Strategy and how that may differ from others and what you bring to your divine client.

Relationships Marketing is looking at the total experience, satisfaction, customer retention and the various communication channels, platforms and frameworks that are not intrusive in nature. The center of your marketing should be around your divine clients because that is what will bring in the meaningful profits and as long as they are experiencing what you are offering you are authentically and extraordinarily serving. Remember, customers only purchase from you once but your divine clients frequently and repeatedly purchase from you, so what you do to keep them engaged is very important. Keeping them engaged in the total experience is what is important especially now with social media platforms, Internet and mobile marketing channels. Relationship marketing really does go way beyond just knowing what their demographics are but actually developing a relationship.

When you are engaging your market, you are looking at the inbound marketing that includes interaction so that they begin to know you more intimately than on the surface because as you build your brand, you must become more intentional about communicating with your clients. It means that with technology has taken over the way that we all communicate going forward and it provides organization and processes that would allow you to stay connected and that gives you many opportunities to share with them exactly who you are and that gives you the open door to be totally authentic and genuinely connect with each client. The communications activities are what keep the client engaged with your programs, teleseminars or any events that you may have planned, not to mention contests. You would need to think outside of the box and become different in your approach now that you have technology at your fingertips. Let's look at some possible Relationship Building Channels that would keep your divine clients engaged but being unique in the approach is up to you because you bring your authentic self, personality and your unique story in which they connect with. There are a few channels that allow you to engage with them and build genuine relationships:

- Social Media
- eNewsletters
- Seminars, Workshops, Trade Shows
- Speaking Engagements
- Community Events
- Charitable Donations
- Referral Programs
- Teleseminars & Webinars
- Alliances with Other Businesses

These are just a few because how you build your relationship marketing strategy should include what you are comfortable with and capable to maintaining. Although, it is a good practice to have at least a minimum of ten channels going on at the same time for effective lead generations. But this must be done with the intentions of being different and unique to grab your divine client's attention. The strategy has to be effective and strong to have a call to action that would warrant a relationship.

Unique Selling Positioning

Your Unique Selling Positioning (USP) is ultimately how your divine clients define you in relation with your competitors and what their perceptions of your particular brand are. Their perception is key to your brand positioning and how it is communicated above your competitor. It really is your own unique expression of what your brand stands for and how it relates to the customer based on the positioning levels: values, benefits and attributes. Your positioning has to be unique and stand out enough where it is distinct in and of itself. The brand and the selling positioning should have value to the target clients and they should immediately know what differentiates you from the rest. Your positioning should be intended for the client to have

> *Your true passion should feel like breathing; it's that natural. – Oprah Winfrey*

obvious value in your product or service. The value is what they will receive such as the benefits that will exceed the cost of your offer. It outweighs what you are selling it for. They have found that your product or service is too valuable to pass up and then benefits are too great to look over. Your benefits are the usefulness of the product or service based on the attributes or features that the product offers. The unique characteristics such as options, features, brand name, product and package design and ultimately the quality of the product or service are the attributes. When designing your Unique Selling Positioning, you would need to be aware of what makes you different from the others or if someone was to copy you, what would they need to do to become totally different. It begins with knowing your product and service inside and out, so intimately so that you can always improve if need be. Find out what makes you unique and upsell that benefit.

Postioning Levels

When you are building your brand, you must know that how you position it is key to your distinction. The positioning of a brand results in a value proposition being presented to the target market and how it is received is based on perception and relevance. There are three types of positioning:

- **Symbolic Position** is based on the characteristics of the brands that enhance the self-esteem of your divine clients. An example, of a dermatologist who enhances physical appearance.

- **Experimental Position** is based on the characteristics of the brands that stimulate sensory or emotional connections with divine clients. An example, a coach seeing the feeling of an Aha moment and joy from a client.

- **Functional Position** is the based on the attributes of products and services and their corresponding benefits and is intended to communicate how divine clients solve their problems or fulfill their needs. An example, high value.

When you know your value and your position in your specific field you are able to see what is valuable to your divine clients. Let's take a look at what you should be asking your clients so that you can maintain your value and continue to enhance it. When you are in business, as an owner and entrepreneur, one should always look for ways to better enhance ways to keep the value meaningful and you do that by asking questions of your clients and doing surveys that give insight on what they want and need offered. You can start by asking:

- What is the true value that you are receiving from me that keeps us working together?
- What is it that you really appreciate about my services or products?
- What would you say are my strengths in how I serve you?
- Do you think that I go beyond my call to serve you or do you feel it could be better?

You have to be willing to ask the hard questions even if you don't want to hear the answers; because that is what it is going to take to serve beyond mediocrity and into excellence. When you as you clients the hard questions, your clients will believe that you do care about how you serve and what you offer is of value. Then because they know that you care, they would be more willing to provide referrals and eventually grow your business. There are great benefits in asking your clients because you can receive testimonials for your marketing collateral and website. It would behoove you to ask the questions that are going to impactful and provide

129

more quality to your service. As a soulful and heart-centered entrepreneur and business owner, you should always be in creative mode that comes straight from the soul because that is where you find a deeper connection to serving your divine clients. There is VALUE that you bring that is different from others and why they want to work with you; therefore, obtaining feedback from them is valuable to you. So listen to the feedback with judge free awareness and do not stay attached to the outcome or the feedback to where you judge yourself. Look at it as positive ways grow your business without offense. What are some values that stand out for you that you connect with and that others will connect with as well? Consider …to name a few!

Values

Accessibility	Competition	Faith	Leadership	Sensitivity
Accountability	Contentment	Family	Love	Significance
Affection	Creativity	Fun	Mindfulness	Spirituality
Ambition	Dependability	Grace	Originality	Strength
Balance	Discipline	Honesty	Perfection	Success
Calmness	Efficiency	Health	Prosperity	Teamwork
Commitment	Excellence	Integrity	Respect	Understanding

Relationship marketing and values go hand-in-hand; therefore, when you are building a brand, know the top five values that you want to grow with. Your values mean a lot to not only you, but it speaks to your divine clients and shares with them who you are. Create and build a relationship branding position with values that grabs attention and establish credibility and trust. Design laser marketing messages that speak directly to clients that you believe to be true for them and what they would find as valuable that gives them a newfound way about themselves and a new way of thinking that creates value for them. This is a unique selling position and sets you apart from your conversation and not be a business that is transactional and not authentic in the approach.

Examples of Laser Marketing Messages That Grab Attention

- As a business coach, I am authentic and committed.
- Your uniqueness brings you joy in your business.
- I value education, so I am going to educate you.
- We are committed to your success.
- Your spirituality will guide you if you allow it to in every aspect of your life.

Your messages are what you believe to be true for you and how you choose to connect with your divine clients and build a relationship on. It should grab their attention and sync with their heartstrings that encourages them to work with you. Share your truth of who you are in your marketing message and relate it to your expertise and your unique offer. After all, they are paying you for your expertise, personality, value and they see your worth. Build a strong brand and relationship marketing message that opens the door to your authentic and extraordinary self.

End of Chapter "Points to Ponder"

1. What makes me different and unique for those who do the same things that I do?

2. How can I make my Personal Brand Statement more about serving than about me?

3. What is the best way for me to build strong professional and lasting relationships?

4. What is my brand position and what does it really stand for?

5. Am I using Functional, Experimental or Symbolic positioning to build my brand?

6. Go ask 10 of your clients to provide feedback to the question... "What value do I or my company bring to your life and business?"

Abundance is not something we acquire. It is something we tune into. There's no scarcity of opportunity to make a living at what you love. There is only a scarcity of resolve to make it happen. — *Wayne Dyer*

Chapter 9 – "Personal Branding Lifestyle"

KEY CHAPTER TOPICS COVERED

- What is Personal Branding Lifestyle
- What Does Your Brand Say About You
- How to market and brand your business

What Is a Personal Branding Lifestyle?

Your Personal Lifestyle Branding is all about you branding yourself in the most effective way that will lend you to the best positive results. Personal Lifestyle Branding is where you are continuously branding your business and you as your brand. Your company begins to become your lifestyle and is known as the work that you love to do and you get paid for it as it becomes integrated into your personal life. It becomes who you are, your identity, your relationships, the interaction and engagement in the community in which you live. Your lifestyle is centered on the company that you have built from the ground up and that is what people know you as. You have become the actual spokesperson for the company with the understanding that all eyes are on you because you are your brand always!

Your Personal Branding Lifestyle is integrated in what you stand for, develops, passion, and is the extension of who you are in your professional and personal life. When you have the personality for what it is that you do, it becomes a part of your brand and often times, more than not, and it precedes you before others meet you. You are your brand and how it is perceived both personally and professionally is totally up to you because you are controlling it; you must understand that anything good or bad is a reflection of you and your business. It becomes connected and intertwined and not separate. There are things that would need to be addressed for damage control just in case there is some negative publicity. Of course you do know that it is better to be prepared than to not be prepared at all.

Building Your Authentic Brand That Speaks For You

What does your brand say about you? Does it speak to your purpose, passion and ideal clients? Is your brand effective, authentic and memorable? Some really don't know and understand how their brand speaks volumes before them and shares with the world who you are and what you do. That is why your personal brand should be authentic. Your brand should be controlled by you and the message that you send out because what you say and how you deliver testifies against your brand. It involves more than what you feel about your business but how others perceive you. Branding includes your marketing message, image, packaging, appearance, personal

> *To let life happen to you is irresponsible.*
> *To create your day is your divine right.*
> — *Ramtha*

selling and the way in which you promote yourself and your business. Building your authentic brand online is a greater challenge to maintain because it is a bigger asset to your brand.

What is an "Authentic Brand"? Designing an authentic brand simply means that you are true to yourself and how you give off your energy about what you do. You speak about your business with passion and clarity, knowing that you are walking in your destiny. Your authentic brand should be clear, reflect who you are, your values, character, uniqueness and pulls from your strengths. Your authentic brand brings your personal and business life together based on your values and your mission in life because you it is who you are. You are building your brand based on your character, values and reflect your genius that you bring to the world. You must get clear on who you are and how you conduct your business knowing that it goes hand-in-hand. Walking in your authenticity sends out positive energy, love and joy in what you do.

When you are designing your authentic personal brand you are really one with who you are and you love you, especially doing what you are most passionate about and how you serve in purpose. Your most authentic self has to have a holistic connection to the love that you have for yourself as you explore self-knowledge. When one loves themselves you become more aware of your strengths, talents, gifts, and your uniqueness because

Your "Authentic Brand Lifestyle" is about who you are and the life that you live.

that is what will connect you to your ideal clients all of the time. It is said that how you treat yourself is how you will treat others, so if you love yourself it would be easy to love others. We are all different and unique in our own special way and that is why a brand should speak to characteristics such as quality, virtue and value. To measure a brand could be simple or complex depending how you would want to measure what your ideal client's connect emotionally. Your true authentic brand needs to attract and hold their attention.

As you create your holistic, organic and authentic brand, you must look at the possible approaches that can expand your brand or hurt your brand. When you hear "Authentic Branding or Marketing" you should always believe they are true to themselves and the world around them because they seek to serve other than money and material gains. Your authentic brand has an emotional connection that allows for your client to trust, know and love you and your brand. It is really about going deep within and seeing what really resonates with you and what does that look and feel like? You are looking at the rawness of who you are and creating a brand that speaks volumes about the real you, your values,

137

your truth, your values, and your unique approach that tells the world how you want to serve them. You are also creating the purest and highest possible belief and creating a life and brand around it. Look at what is your highest vision that you can customize that totally flows through you and breathes your passion and purpose. It must vibrate deeply in your soul to have a pure connection for you to follow and for others to believe in your brand.

When you begin the process, there a few steps that you must take in order to prepare for building your authentic brand because you will use it as a roadmap to follow. It sets the model by which you will always conduct your business. The initial steps are as follow:

1. You must begin to convey what your personal desires are.
2. Your Personal Brand should express and communicate the real "You".
3. Understand how to execute and incorporate your Personal Brand into your life and your business.

With these three questions it begins the journey of creating a *Personal Dream, Personal Purpose Statement, Personal Intentions and Goals, and your Authentic Personal Brand Statement.* Let me define each for you so that it can push you on your journey.

- **Personal Dream** – Write your personal dream down by including what brings you joy, who you are, what you want to become, your vision and knowledge behind what you will bring to the brand. Also include a financial goal that would make your dream a reality.

- **Personal Purpose Statement** – Write one sentence that shares your ultimate purpose for you and your business.

- **Personal Intentions and Goals** – What are your intentions and commitments to achieving your goals? What goals are you seriously committing to that shares your personal brand for your business?

- **Authentic Personal Brand Statement** – You are going to share what your brand stands for and what you will accomplish, your promise and what you will be dedicated to in your holistic business.

As you work on these four areas, you will begin to look at what really matters to you and your business. You are designing the brand and how you want your ideal clients to perceive your brand and also how memorable your brand can be. It includes your own uniqueness, meaning, and most of all how inspiring your brand is. Your brand would be heartfelt and soul-filled based how you will provide excellence to your clients. Your business should represent the harmony between you and your business. Therefore, spend some time thinking about this because it will follow you going forward, so it is very important. I suggest that you get in a quiet place or outside with nature to get still and listen to your soul and what you are feeling. You must go deep within and become inspired by what resonates with you.

When you are developing your thoughts around your brand you must look both internally and externally. Internally, you are looking at what you feel inside and how you can be centered in how you want to attribute your brand to the good of the world. What objectives, goals and actions that you want to accomplish with your authentic brand with how they are the focal point of all the behaviors? Your brand once it is defined internally, it is so empowering and it resonates with your ideal client because they feel the authenticity of your brand and hopefully keeps them loyal. However, there are many deliverables that would need to be incorporated to keep them loyal. Yet, it is your personal ambition that would keep them engaged and sustained so that building your brand begins to grow organically.

Externally, your brand should capture your ideal client's positive emotional reactions and speaks to their needs and wants. When you are looking at your brand externally, you are paying attention to the colors, logo, slogan and symbols that represent you. Additionally, there are other factors included such as: your story, location,

> *If you do what you've always done, you'll get what you've always gotten. - Anthony Robbins*

approachability, engagement and also receiving feedback from your clients for better development and improvement without offense. As a business owner you know what it feels like internally but you have to be able to communicate that to the world and based on how they perceive you through consistent improvement. It is good to place yourself in your client's seat and look from the outside in without your own judgment.

What Do You Want Your Authentic Brand to Stand For?

Your "Authentic Brand" states who you are and translating your vision, goals and objectives that are based on your own personal ambition. All of which are balanced and in alignment with values, emotions, spiritual, and more holistic view. Your brand is a promise as to what you will deliver and it is consistently maintained to grow the brand and the perceptions around it. So you would need to begin with what are the intentions, soul and personal commitment for your brand.

Your brand means a lot in how you put it out to world such as:

- Brand Values
- Brand Personality
- Brand Message
- Brand Energy
- Brand Colors
- Brand Profitability
- Brand Logo, Trade lines & Taglines
- Brand Visibility & Marketing

Therefore, in order to build a strong and memorable brand that is positioned and stabilized, all of the elements must mesh together in order to create a sustainable branding and message. It all takes so much to create a brand that can last a very long time. The purpose of having an authentic brand is so that you are true to it and yourself and others would respect it. Your personal brand speaks volumes of you and how you conduct business.

When you are preparing your authentic marketing message and brand you want your brand to constantly deliver quality, performance, and also what it promises. The brand should have the strength behind it to stand the test of time and the structure and process to do what it will provide. As you build your brand, there should be some type of measurement process in place to consistently track and measure how the brand and marketing message is attracting and sustaining the market. A business should always be testing and asking their clients through perhaps a survey as to how did they hear about the company? What attracted them to the brand and what would they prefer to become loyal to the brand; just to name a few. The authentic brand and marketing message should be constant in what is sending out into the world.

An authentic brand should build creditability in terms of partnering with other brands that can create a win-win for both parties involved and not only the main parties but also the community. It also includes building relationships with non-profit organizations, sponsoring credible events and raising donations that would give back for a good cause. It creates the brand loyalty among the customers or clients and gets them to stay connected and engaged without mimics and gimmicks to keep them. That is not authentic because being authentic means that you're true and pure in what you deliver and it is heart-centered and soul-focused.

Additionally, as individuals and companies follow you, there is a specific marketing message that sets you apart and they can grasp exactly what you offer and how you intend to provide a service, product, or solution to a need or want. How would you connect with them and what does that look like for you?

You Are Your Brand So Wear It Well!

Building a brand is a task in and of itself, especially when you are starting from the beginning, because people don't know you and they would have to hear your name and brand several times in order to remember what you do exactly. Your brand is "You" and as you build it there are many things to consider as you build authentically. Look at Oprah, Donald Trump, Prince, and even Michael Jackson who are all a name-brand household names that grab the attention of those who know them. They had to build their brand from the ground up and some did not have the means to put into their brand as some may have the resources to do. Yet, when building the brand, it becomes a way of influence and sometimes clout depending on the industry. Their personal brands brought about a certain recognition that is based on the perception of how people feel when they encounter the name. But what makes them different? Who are they really when you only see them in the spotlight and you are not with them at all times? However, you are with you all of the time. You are your brand!

What does that really mean to you? It means that as your build a successful brand, it will become more about you, your service, product or solution that you bring to the world to serve. There are a lot of individuals who want to build a personal brand; however, they don't know all of the intricacies that go into building such. When building a personal authentic brand one must first understand that you are putting yourself in the spotlight and stepping on stage to say to the world "Here I Am. This is ME!" You are out there and you are bringing what your brand promises.

Your personal authentic brand will be based on the way that you are able to control your brand and the perception that you want for others to perceive you. Perhaps we are all our personal brands that we live everyday based on the way we live and others perceive you. The personal authentic brand includes:

- Your dress (Yes! What you were everyday)
- Where you live

- What kind of car you drive
- How You Speak
- Where you frequent as of stores, restaurants
- Who are your network of friends, colleagues, and family
- What school you attended
- And other things that you would not think about

All of which are not mentioned but you get the picture. It does matter when you are building a brand that has intentions of having a strong brand equity that will last. Building a personal brand is organic and not done overnight so it does take time to massage and grow because you are talking about a business that will last for generations to come hopefully. When you are building a soulful brand, it takes heart and great intentions on how it is perceived and your divine client's perceptions are what makes the difference and unique in their eyes as you build a relationship with them.

You and Your Business are "1"

When you started your business, you started it with a reason and a purpose in mind and yes that is to make money, but as a soul-centered business, it goes much deeper than that. For you and me it is more about serving and as you take on your business's identity, you become one with it because it is embedded in your spirit and deep in your soul. You begin to live it, dream about it, breathe it and love it daily so it is a part of who you are. It is about sharing with the world humbly and in servitude saying "Here is who I am". Your faith in what you believe when you show up is who you are at the core and that is what reverberates with your brand. It is being honest and soulful to speak with your clients on heart-felt marketing and branding. Your brand creates for you exactly who you are and how you are able to stand up in your brand and walk in that daily.

When you are one with your brand, you **connect in a way** that you are living, breathing, and showing up in the world that fills your soul and increases your faith to go higher. You are being totally present in the here and now with your brand and everything you do; you are living your brand and doing business from a place of heart-centered and soulful living.

End of Chapter "Points to Ponder"

1. What is unique about your brand?

2. What values, benefits and attributes do you offer consistently?

3. What are your personal brand intentions and goals?

4. What is my personal branding lifestyle represent?

5. What do I want my brand to stand for, for generations to come?

Chapter 10 – Authentic Marketing Attraction Tools

Key Chapter Topics Covered

- Understanding Your Inner Awareness
- Mantras That Change Your Mindset
- Visualizations, Meditations & Declarations

Client Attraction Tools

In order to live your EXTRAORDINARY Life NOW! You must begin thinking differently than what you have been so that you can start doing the action to get to where you want to be. Sometimes, or let me just speak for me, I have had to work hard on changing my thoughts because there have been many times where I had thoughts of self-defeat and I had to change my mindset around in order to begin the life that I have always dreamed of as a business woman and have the lifestyle that was burning inside of me. I have spoken with many people and even clients who were in the same stuck mindset and was asked over and over, how do I get out of this dark cloud and into the abundance in my mind that I know to be.

You have to change your thoughts, actions and the way you move forward in your business and in life if you want to live an extraordinary life and build a personal branding lifestyle that speaks to whom you really are. I have added some daily practices, mantras and affirmations that I have used to change my mind to keep me focused on building a successful business and brand that I have always dreamed of and desired. I believe this for you too. I believe that your dreams are inside of you waiting to be explored and blossomed into what is supposed to be. NOW IS THE TIME TO LIVE *AUTHENTICALLY!*

Inner Awareness

Your Inner Awareness that you seeking is all on the inside of you, you just have to find it. This is what is called soul-searching and really understanding what you need to know to speak you and walk in your own divine truth. You are who you are and these tools are here to assist you in finding out who you are from your core with judge-free awareness.

First Things First – Inner Work

- Know Yourself – Boundaries, Likes, Dislikes, Your Truth

- Know What You Need and Ask For It –

- Find Your Authentic Voice

- Know What Your Purpose Is and

- Be Willing To Invest In Doing The Work

- Know What Your Faith Means To You

- Become Aware of Your New Consciousness

- Believing In A Higher Source Than Yourself

- Walk In Your Divine Pathway

Then Next Things – Outer Work

- Know That You Are Your Brand and You Wear It Everyday

- How You Dress, Drive, Live all speak your Authentic **Brand**

- Authentic Business Branding Principles that Speak Your Message

- Know Your Authentic Marketing Message that Speaks Who You Are

- Build a Business Legacy with Great Foundation and Purpose

- All Marketing and Branding Collateral Speaks the Same Message

Daily Practice

- Find your quite place in your home or out in nature.

- Clothes your eyes and take a few deep breaths.

- Clear your mind of every thought.

- Sit in an open position that allows you to take deep long breaths.

- Sit in silence for a minimum of 15 minutes and be still.

- Be with your thoughts and let them go.

- Journal your thoughts daily.

- Keep a "Gratitude" Journal to write down what you are grateful for daily.

- Speak soft and speak your truth to yourself daily.

- Look in the mirror and tell yourself: "I am good and all good things come to be." Or other affirmations that you like.

- Be with nature daily by taking a 10 minute walk. Or sit in the park.

- Be thankful for all good and bad experiences that you may have.

Money Mantras

- Money flows to me openly and freely.

- I am open to all sources of money.

- I am a money magnet and money finds its way to me.

- Money follows me all of the days of my life.

- I am blessed with an abundant flow of money.

- I am a powerful money magnet.

- The universe provides everything that I need.

- Money comes to me effortlessly.

- Money comes to me in surprising and fun ways.

- Money always comes to me with perfect timing.

- There are no limits on what I am expecting.

- Today I release my fears, blocks and negative energy on money.

- I can feel my money abundance flowing to me freely.

- I am aligned to receive my abundance breakthrough.

- I choose faith over my money starting right now.

Abundance Declarations

- Abundance is around me, abundance is within me, abundance is through me.

- I am willing to be more abundant now.

- Abundance flows easily when I am relaxed.

- This day is filled with endless expressions of abundance.

- Today I will expand my awareness of the abundance around me and everyone I come into contact with.

- I always have more than enough.

- I am open to new abundance every day.

- Thank You for my great abundance daily.

- I allow the universe and my God of abundance to bless me daily.

- I am grateful for my life and everything in it.

- My heart is grateful and draws more to me.

- I am blessed and highly favored.

- Life loves me and I love life.

Client Attraction Declarations

- ♩ My divine clients come to me effortlessly.

- ♩ My divine clients are attracted to what I have to offer.

- ♩ My divine clients are able to pay me what I am worth.

- ♩ My divine clients value what I offer and the universe supports me.

- ♩ My divine clients are seeking me out.

- ♩ My divine clients appreciate how I serve them.

- ♩ My divine clients are connected to my soul and what is inside of me.

- ♩ My divine clients are connected to my purpose and walk the same pathway.

- ♩ My divine clients are living in abundance

- ♩ I love working with my divine clients.

- ♩ I visualize success for me and my divine clients.

- ♩ I am grateful for serving my divine clients.

Energy Meditations

- Everything is energy.

- Every object that you see or feel around us is nothing but energy.

- Focus mentally on details and put positive energy around and through it.

- Riches, mediocrity, and poverty begin in the mind.

- A positive attitude brings strength, energy and initiative

- Positive thing is expecting, visualizing and talking with faith and certainty that you will receive what you want.

- When you say "I Can" and you expect things to show up, you shall have.

- When you place positive energy out, you will receive positive back.

- Clear and concise thoughts produce clear and concise results.

- Train you mind to think "positive" and change your mindset.

- Happy thoughts attract happy people.

- When you change to thinking positive thoughts, your life will begin to change in that manner as well.

- You should repeat inspiring and positive quotes and affirmations daily and sometimes 2-3 times a day depending on your mindset.

Visualization of a Successful Business

- Visualize what your lifestyle would be like if money and time were not an option.

- Visualize what your authentic business would look like and what your brand would stand for.

- Design a vision board that you are able to see on a daily basis to keep your dreams before you.

- Never stop dreaming, fanaticizing about where you want to be then take action steps to get there.

- Change your thoughts and change your reality

- Visualize details and give positive energy to what you see your divine clients looking like.

- Visualize what a successful business looks like for you. (Revenue, # of Employees, # of locations, etc.)

- Visualize what joyful days are working for yourself looks and feels like.

- Visualize the lifestyle you would like to live and how does that feel.

"I Am" Declarations

- ♒ I AM Forward to a Great Future in My Business!

- ♒ I AM Successful in My Business!

- ♒ I AM Living My Life's Purpose

- ♒ I AM Healthy!

- ♒ I AM Living Abundantly!

- ♒ I AM Living my Best Life NOW!

- ♒ I AM Living Authentically!

- ♒ I AM Dreaming BIG!

- ♒ I AM Blessed!

- ♒ I AM Fruitful!

- ♒ I AM Thankful!

- ♒ I AM Grateful!

- ♒ I AM Anointed!

- ♒ I AM Always in High Spirits!

- ♒ I AM Expecting Greatness!

- ♒ I AM Confident, Secure, Talented and Valuable!

- ♒ I AM Living Boldly!

Building Your Authentic Brand

- Know who you are inside and out

- Wear your brand daily

- Build your lifestyle around your brand

- Walk in positive energy at all times

- Learn how to respond and not react

- Always be totally true to yourself regardless

- Be who you are and not who others want you to be

- Find your purpose and walk into your destiny

- Create a brand that speaks to your soul and connects with others

- Be consistent!

- Stay in contact with all potential and present clients

- Always seek to go the extra mile in service

- Personalize your brand and service

- Show appreciation to everyone (clients, employees, potential clients, etc.)

- Choose employees that represent your brand as you would

- Be conscious of what you say, do, and how you treat others

- Stay true to your business, purpose and passion

- Build a client loyalty program

- Provide irresistible offers for referrals

- Create an Authentic Affiliate Program

- Speak and Live an Authentic Branding Lifestyle

Trust Life and Believe!

It is my clear intentions to bring you content that you can use to assist in implementing your own Authentic Brand that shares who you are with the world and the divine clients that you were called her to serve. Your marketing mindset must shift from transactional marketing to divine relationship and draw on what is in your soul so that you brand truly represents who you are as an authentic business owner and entrepreneur. There is a shift in the atmosphere about how business has been done to what it should look like. Not just with the technology and social media but because small businesses has become the backbone of sustaining the economy and in order for them to be sustained it has to shift from being about "ME, ME, ME" but what you have inside of you that you need to give yourself away to serve.

The words transformation and authentic has been thrown around so loosely that others cannot tell who is authentic or not because of the unethical, greedy marketing tactics that continue to pull at your divine clients and not enhancing their lives and businesses in a manner that is totally and completely authentic, sincere, genuine and honest. It is time out for doing business practices the way it has been done. So I hope that this book in some way has helped you change your mind set about authentic marketing and branding in order to grow your business. Your business will not necessarily grow over night, but it is possible if everything is in alignment but you must do business the right way and do right by others in order to live in truth and authenticity. The transformational shift must occur about your branding, marketing and understand that your lifestyle is intertwined in it. Go Build Your Authentic Business…I Believe In You!

I totally believe that when you change your mind set and consciousness to what you desire and will in your life, you begin to receive it. I know that once I begin to get really clear on what I wanted in my life and what I did not want to attract, I stopped thinking about it and giving it power. I begin to think positive even when things in my life were all going wrong. I had to change a lot of my associations and some of them were really close, but I had to love me more and I had to want success bad enough because I was not going anywhere if I stayed around negative energy. It is crucial to change your environment to that which is totally supportive of who you are and what you want to do. Energy is powerful and when you are conscious of how you send it out, you are able to attract what you want whether positive or negative. If you want to attract great things in your life then you must give off that positive energy to receive it.

That is the same way in the *Authentic Marketing Attraction*™ *Program* that I offer and teach because if you are clear on who you want to work with, you will attract them because your authentic marketing voice and message are clear and the energy that you put out makes the attraction because your souls and spirits are connected and the universe supports the connection. In an authentic, soulful, heart-centered business, you are completely walking in your truth and sending out the energy to those whom you are called to serve. You are being your best self and walking in your divine purpose to attract those who are supposed to work with you. It is a win-win for both and that makes it all natural and not push and pull.

As an Authentic Marketing Master, it took me a while to get to this sacred place and space that I am in and I must say that it feels truly amazing because I get to be exactly who I am in my business and work with only my divine clients and have fun doing it. For myself it has taken me many hurdles to get over to get to this place such as this. I have looked at it as life's lesson on my journey to be the best that I am called to be. The journey is one that looking back; I had to travel because each lesson was a stepping stone to something greater. I realized that I had to go through the broke phase, growing stages and everything in between to get to where I am today. All of our businesses will grow, evolve and change over time and it is up to you to change with it, hopefully for the better.

As you walk on your path to your authentic self and in your unique business that only you can do the way that you can do it, you will begin to see your true self and exactly what you need to offer and serve the world. You are special and unique doing what you are called to do and to be in the world; therefore, you should accept your gifts, talents, and expertise so that you can birth all that is within you. What is in you has to get out in order to live your life on purpose and that is why I love what I do because once my clients learn what their purpose is, I get to assist them designing an authentic marketing message around it and that is what excites me and motivates me because I get to watch other people's dreams be birthed and walked out; which is so exciting to me. I am blessed and grateful to be living me purpose and passion. I want to help you live yours, so let's be authentic and stand up in our truth to live the *EXRAORDINARY* and *EXCELLENT* LIFE THAT WE WERE BORN TO LIVE! MUCH SUCCESS TO YOU!

One-Page Marketing Plan

Business:

_____

_____

Mission/Vision Statement:

_____

_____

_____

_____

Personal Brand Statement:

_____

_____

_____

Divine Clients:

_____

_____

_____

Services / Products:

_____

_____

_____

Authentic Marketing Strategies:

_____

_____

_____

Weekly Action Plan:

_____

_____

_____

Lifestyle Branding & Marketing

Questions to Ponder To For Authentic Marketing & Branding:

What is your "Authentic Marketing Message" that you want to share with the world?

_____

_____

_____

_____

_____

_____

What does your brand say about "you"?

_____

_____

_____

_____

What is your purpose, passion and pursuit in your business?

_____

_____

_____

_____

What is your grand vision and how does it serve the world?

_____

_____

_____

_____

_____

_____

_____

_____

What are you called to do to play BIGGER in the world?

_____
_____
_____
_____
_____

How are you called to serve them (divine clients)?

_____
_____
_____
_____
_____
_____

What does "Conscious-Centered Business, Soulful, Heart-Centered" business mean to you?

_____
_____
_____
_____
_____
_____

If you had the opportunity to live your most authentic life and stand up in your truth, what would it look like?

_____
_____
_____
_____
_____
_____
_____
_____
_____
_____
_____

What is God's vision for your life? Not your vision, but your Higher Calling's vision?

_____

_____

_____

_____

_____

What am I willing to give up, to follow my passion and live my "EXTRAORDINARY SELF"?

_____

_____

_____

_____

_____

What is holding me back from living my extraordinary life that I know that I am called to live?

_____

_____

_____

_____

_____

My Action Plans To Build My Authentic Brand & Extraordinary Life

_____

_____

_____

_____

_____

_____

_____

_____

HOW TO DEVELOP YOUR BRANDING STRATEGIES AND OBJECTIVES

Before you begin to develop your marketing strategies and objectives it is important that a cross-representation—those with varied skills hired to perform different tasks or responsibilities—of your staff spend some time carefully examining the following:

1. **The clarity of your mission**—your staff and your clients should know who you are, what you do, how long you have been doing what you do, why you exist, and be able to share this information clearly and succinctly.

2. **The products and services your business offers**—all of your products should be well known by your staff in addition to the unique niche that your organization has compared to your competitors.

3. **The target clients for these products and services and their particular needs and expectations**—this information may be gained through surveys and small group discussions with the clients you currently serve as well as those you wish to serve.

4. **The competitors in your community and the products and services offered by these competitors**—to know your competition is to know your opponent and how to position your organization so that you stay a step ahead of that competition.

5. **The amount of funds that your organization will dedicate to its marketing strategies and objectives and how you will monitor and evaluate the results of those strategies and objectives**—your marketing strategies should be reflected as a line item in your budget.

Your authentic marketing strategies and objectives could include some of the following approaches that will allow you to take your services to a broad range of probable clients and the timeframes to accomplish the outlined strategies:

- Branding your organization with its unique logo or motto;
- Keeping your logo in front of the public through tangible promotional items that have a long- and repeat-use life, e.g., coffee mugs, key chains and calendars;
- Designing, enhancing and updating your web site on a regular basis;
- Speaking on your local radio or television station;
- Writing a monthly column in your local community newspaper;
- Sponsoring a sports team at your local school;
- Distributing fliers and other written communications to small businesses and churches in your communities;
- Publishing a monthly e-newsletter for circulation to your customers and residents;
- Hosting an Annual Open House or Holiday Event for your customers, friends, funders and probable new funders;

- Supporting other products and services—authors, artists and workshop presenters by sponsoring events around their expertise at your organization; and
- Staying visible through attending conferences and other networking opportunities to learn about new products and services.

HOW TO POSITION AND PROTECT YOUR BRAND IN THE MARKETPLACE

- When building your authentic brand, it is consistent in delivering results.

- It must be measureable and receives the consistency of deliverables that is constant with your authenticity.

- Your authentic brand has processes, systems and structures in place that allows you to bring about what your brand promises.

- Your authentic brand must stand for something; therefore, what is your brand known for in the community? What strategic alliances are you in relation with that build your brand?

- What does your brand fulfill in the community socially? In other words, what networks, relationships and allies are all winnable?

- Your divine clients know and understand exactly what you have to offer and how you are here to serve them. What does that look like for you, your brand and the divine clients you want to serve?

- What do you want you divine clients to clearly articulate about what it is that you offer and how you serve?

- Build a brand that speaks to who you are and without compromise because you are your brand.

- Your authentic brand should walk the talk and stand for something...have meaning and value.

- Take pride in your own brand because it is all that you have along with your word.

- Watch what is mentioned about you both online and offline. Set up Google Alerts so that anytime your name or business goes on the Internet, you will know.

- Have a brand crisis management process in case something does happen and you need to respond and not react to damage control.

Elyshia Brooks.com

About The Author

Elyshia Brooks

As the Founder-President/CEO, Elyshia Brooks, Inc. and Kreative Group, Inc., she is a professional marketing and business coachsultant who develops and implements marketing strategies and solutions to assist businesses and organizations in achieving their marketing & sales goals and objectives.

Elyshia's 20 years of the marketing industry career includes direct marketing, public relations, marketing and business strategy, advertising, brand management and event planning. Elyshia earned her bachelor's degree in Marketing from Albany State University and her MBA in Marketing from Strayer University. She is currently a doctoral candidate at Walden University pursuing a D.B.A. in Marketing and Business Strategy to be completed in Fall 2013.

Elyshia specializes in small business growth, relationship marketing, branding, public relations and marketing strategies. Her expertise includes business and marketing plan development, lean marketing plans, asset management and building business credit. She also works with busy professional women who are looking for more meaningful and balanced lives.

As a consultant / coach, Elyshia uses her experience to provide solutions for maximizing performance. Her mission is to assist clients discover solutions that work so they have time, energy, and space for what matters most. As a success-oriented business coach, she works with individuals from the highest levels of corporate life every day – helping them achieve a more successful business and well-rounded life.

Kreative Group, Inc. specializes in marketing and business strategy, brand management for small to midsize companies, and non-profit organizations. She believes that marketing education is an integral part in the development and success of a successful business or organization; therefore, she travels conducting marketing and branding workshops and seminars across the country.

Elyshia has founded Elyshia Brooks International, Inc. (www.ElyshiaBrooks.com) where she will travel globally coaching, consulting and training other entrepreneurs and small business owners in Authentic Marketing Strategies and growing into a multi-million dollar business. She also is a professor at two local community colleges and will be teaching at additional colleges and universities in the fall.

Attend an Authentic Marketing Attraction™ Seminar

Your business needs a new Marketing Makeover and NOW is the time. Your spirit resonated with what I mentioned in the book and if you would like to attend one of my seminars, workshops, conferences, retreats or perhaps one-on-one private coaching…You Can!

They are impactful with relevant content, customized strategies for your specific business and a creative way to build your authentic brand and marketing campaign. You know that you need a change and your soul is crying out on to work with your divine clients which whom you will be most happy working with, but you may be stuck. After attending one of my events not only your business will be revived but your spirit will to and they are all connected to have a soulful business that is destined for purpose, wealth and abundance.

To Attend an

Authentic Marketing Attraction™ Seminar

Authentically Branding the Extraordinary "ME" Tour

In an area near you, please visit:

www.ElyshiaBrooks.com

To Reach Elyshia and Her Team

Elyshia and her team are excellent in capturing the essence of what your soul-brand means and stands for along with creating a marketing message that speaks directly to your divine clients that you are supposed to be serving. You will not regret working with her as she has insight on bringing the best in you out and capturing your true passion so that you can get paid what you are worth and having fun doing it. Elyshia offers three significant programs:

- **Authentic Marketing Attraction™ Program** – a program that is impact with content to get you attracting your divine clients consistently.

- **Elyshia's Elite Circle™** - is uniquely designed to helping you propel both your business and life into new heights – for those who may believe that they are on a mission to catapult their business and lifestyle.

- **Authentic Marketing Mastery™** - Private 1-on-1 Coaching with weekly accountability, two retreats (Spring & Fall). And so much more.

My team and I would love to have a conversation and perhaps meet with you to discuss the success of your business. Your purpose and passion needs to be walked out and you know that you cannot do it by doing what you have always done. Now is the time. Email me and my team at Elyshia@ElyshiaBrooks.com for scheduling a 30-Minute Discovery Session visit http://www.ElyshiaBrooks.com

I Am Waiting To Serve You!

Elyshia Brooks International, Inc.
Authentic Services

INNER TRANSFORMATION
Success Coaching
Goal Setting & Purpose Design
Inner Beauty Transformation
Purpose, Passion and Pathway
Authentic Living & Lifestyle

OUTER – BUSINESS TRANSFORMATION
Authentic Marketing Coaching
Authentic Branding Coaching
Authentic Business Design
Marketing Money Mindset

LIFESTYLE TRANSFORAMTION
Success Mastery
Living on Top

Thank you for entrusting your time, business and success in my hands for the time we have shared. Please remember that I am not successful until you are. I am here to push you into greatness. Success in Him Always!

Elyshia Brooks, MBA, CEO/President
Elyshia Brooks International, Inc. ~ Authentic Marketing Institute ~
Kreative Group, Inc.

Special Thanks To:

Special Thank You to all of those who have assisted me with making this first book project a success. From the bottom of my heart, I really appreciate you, your authenticity, prayers and positive energy. To my clients that have worked with me and have allowed me to grow, educate, engage, and empower not only you, but myself because you gave me a chance to walk out my destiny and passion.

My Spiritual Father, Bishop Terrell L. Murphy, Senior Pastor New Birth-Charlotte; for speaking life into me weekly and who has pushed me into my extraordinary self!

Cover Design by Leah Ponds Art Studio. www.LeahPonds.com. Leah you are amazing and talented. God has given you a gift that is and will be a blessing to all who encounter you. Thank you for my amazing book cover and marketing materials.

Pamela Gibson at Because of You Hair Salon, thank you for making me beautiful constantly. I not only appreciate your gifted hands but also your authentic friendship. I love you!

Ebony Alexander of J&E Photography; you were amazing and I so love your work and your spirit. Continue to walk in your destiny and all that God has for you.

19103107R00099

Made in the USA
Charleston, SC
07 May 2013